FINANCING
THE
1988
ELECTION

FINANCING THE 1988 ELECTION

HERBERT E. ALEXANDER
University of Southern California

MONICA BAUER
Western New England College

WESTVIEW PRESS
Boulder • San Francisco • Oxford

Copyright © 1991 by Westview Press, Inc.

Published in 1991 in the United States of America by Westview Press, Inc., 5500 Central Avenue, Boulder, Colorado 80301, and in the United Kingdom by Westview Press, 36 Lonsdale Road, Summertown, Oxford OX2 7EW

Library of Congress Cataloging-in-Publication Data
Alexander, Herbert E.
    Financing the 1988 election / Herbert E. Alexander and Monica Bauer.
        p. cm.
    Includes bibliographical references and index.
    ISBN 0-8133-8268-8. — ISBN 0-8133-8269-6 (pbk.)
    1. Campaign funds—United States. 2. Presidents—United States—Election—1988. 3. United States. Congress—Elections, 1988.
I. Bauer, Monica. II. Title.
JK1991.A6855 1991
324.7′8′097309048—dc20   91-6727
                                                                               CIP

Printed and bound in the United States of America

∞   The paper used in this publication meets the requirements
     of the American National Standard for Permanence of Paper
     for Printed Library Materials Z39.48-1984.

10   9   8   7   6   5   4   3   2   1

CONTENTS

TABLES

PREFACE AND ACKNOWLEDGMENTS

In this eighth quadrennial book on the financing of presidential election campaigns, the research and analytical techniques used previously were reexamined, and considerable modifications were made to accommodate the new data. The 1988 elections constituted the fourth experience with public funding, adding new dimensions and leading to new ways of dealing with and thinking about the subject. Each successive study is an educational experience, and the 1988 campaign was notable in the diversity of ways and means found to raise, handle, and spend the large amounts of money used.

A new agency, the Federal Election Commission (FEC), came into being in 1975, producing immense amounts of data and information and affecting greatly the contours and analyses of the 1988 study. Some amounts reported in this book as spent by a given candidate may differ from other figures because audit totals of the FEC do not agree with totals in its published compilations or with direct or later information that the Citizens' Research Foundation (CRF) received. The CRF made certain adjustments that the FEC did not. Closing dates for some CRF analyses differed from those in FEC or other compilations, thus resulting in different totals. A number of definitions of categories differ, affecting which groups are included or excluded in certain totals. And for some purposes, soft money, independent expenditures, compliance costs, and communication costs were included, unlike compilations by others. Moreover, the FEC compilations often give totals only for general election candidates, going back to January 1 of the election year or previous year, without separating primary election from general election spending and not accounting for the totals of dollars raised and spent by primary election losers. Of course, the FEC disclosure forms are not designed to differentiate accurately between primary election and general election spending.

So many events and facts required description independently by topic that it was difficult to organize the book efficiently. There would have been so many notes cross-referencing topics such as fund-raising or public financing within the confines of the book that, for the most part, we dispensed with these. Accordingly, readers should use both the Table of Contents and the Index for cross-referencing.

This study attempts to update and to keep active analyses and categories of data developed over the years by Professors James Pollock, Louise Overacker, and Alexander Heard; the Senate Subcommittee on Privileges and Elections (under the chairmanship of Senator Albert Gore of Tennessee) in 1956; and the seven previous volumes authored or coauthored by Herbert E. Alexander in his series on finance and elections.

ACKNOWLEDGMENTS

The data in this study were collected by the CRF. An early analysis was published in a brief article by Herbert E. Alexander, "The Price We Pay for Our Presidents," *Public Opinion,* vol. 11, no. 6, March/April, 1989, pp. 46–48. Special appreciation is due to many individuals for providing information in personal interviews, through correspondence, and by telephone. Many finance managers and others preferred to remain anonymous. Because it would be unfair to name some and not others, we regretfully do not list the many persons in such capacities who graciously cooperated.

We acknowledge the help of Rebecca Herrick, a graduate student at the University of Nebraska, for her assistance with data from the University of Michigan National Election Survey.

Monica Bauer did not participate in the writing of "Epilogue: Shaping Election Reform" and does not have any responsibility for its contents or conclusions. Special thanks are due to David Beiler for his comprehensive research on election reform and his editing of the Epilogue.

Throughout, CRF's assistant director, Gloria Cornette, was a constant source of strength, managing superbly the preparation of the manuscript at all stages, typing under deadline, and preparing the index.

None of those who were so helpful is responsible for errors of omission or commission; for those, as for interpretations, we bear sole responsibility. We appreciate the cooperation and encouragement received from officers and members of the board of trustees of the Citizens'

Research Foundation, but the presentation is ours and does not necessarily reflect their views.

We are especially grateful for a generous grant from the Amoco Foundation, enabling this volume to be prepared. Without the contributions of numerous additional supporters of the Citizens' Research Foundation, this study would not have been possible.

Herbert E. Alexander
Monica Bauer

INTRODUCTION

In 1988, George Bush won the presidential election with 426 electoral votes in forty states, while Michael Dukakis won in ten states and the District of Columbia, receiving 111 electoral votes; 1 electoral vote was cast for Senator Lloyd Bentsen, the Democratic vice presidential candidate. With a voter turnout of 50.1 percent, the Democrats retained their majority in both the U.S. Senate and the House.

Developments in financing the 1988 election campaigns were notable in many ways, although they generally have received far less systematic attention than other aspects of the elections. Accordingly, these developments are the subject of this book. Campaign money may be conceived of as a tracer element in politics; much valuable information about the patterns of political events and results and the distribution of political power may be obtained by following the path of money through the course of election campaigns.

During the 1987–1988 election cycle, total political campaign spending at all levels—national, state, and local—exceeded $2.7 billion, a 50 percent increase over the estimated political spending bill in the previous presidential election cycle. Although the $2.7 billion figure indicates that campaign spending continues to grow at a rate greater than that of inflation, the increase over the corresponding 1984 figure also is due in part to the fact that more complete information is available regarding campaign costs.

The 1988 national elections were the seventh to be conducted under the Federal Election Campaign Act (FECA) and its 1974 amendments, and the presidential election was the fourth conducted under the system of public funding initiated by the act and its companion legislation. Although the FECA was enacted in part to control campaign spending, which had reached unprecedented levels in the 1972 presidential campaigns, more than one-half of the $2.7 billion campaign expenditure total in 1988 was used to influence federal election results. The cost of the items and services many federal campaigns must purchase, including media broadcast time, air travel, telephones, and the specialized expertise of campaign consultants, rose dramatically. Candidates and their supporters responded by adopting some previously used methods of raising and spending funds and devising various new means, some of which provoked controversy in the midst of the campaigns and triggered demands for further campaign finance regulation.

In the chapters that follow, developments in financing the 1984 election campaigns are described and analyzed. This focus is not intended to slight the numerous nonfinancial factors that influenced the 1988 election results. Indeed, political party rules, national and local issues, the prestige of office and advantages of incumbency, leadership and communication skills, the composition of election districts, and the mood of the electorate all played important roles in determining election outcomes. But it is campaign money, as the late historian and journalist Theodore H. White pointed out, that enables candidates to purchase items and services needed to influence party rules, to make their views on issues known, to gain office and demonstrate their communication skills, and to sway the electorate. "Money buys attention," he wrote. "It buys . . . television and radio time; it buys expertise, computers, organization, travel, visuals for the evening news."[1] By shedding light on these and other uses of campaign money and clarifying its relationships with other factors that help determine election results, we hope to illuminate the political process and contribute to the understanding of political influence and power in the United States.

NOTES

1. Theodore H. White, *America in Search of Itself* (New York: Harper and Row, 1982), p. 426.

$1

SPENDING IN THE
1988 ELECTIONS

During the 1987–1988 election cycle, political candidates and committees, and organizations and individuals hoping to influence the electoral process and election results spent $2.7 billion on political campaigns. This spending covered not only campaigns for nomination and election to federal offices—the presidency, vice presidency, and seats in the houses of Congress—but also nomination and election campaigns for state and local offices, campaigns for and against ballot propositions, efforts by numerous independent organizations to register and turn out voters, and the costs of administering national, state, and local political party organizations and numerous interest and ideological group-sponsored political committees.

The $2.7 billion represents an increase of 50 percent over the corresponding Citizens' Research· Foundation (CRF) estimate for the 1983–1984 election cycle. This increase exceeded notably the 13.5 percent rise in the Consumer Price Index during the four-year period from January 1, 1984, to January 1, 1988, thereby stoking the fires of criticism regarding political campaign costs. Critics maintain that high campaign costs force candidates to devote an inordinate amount of time to raising money. They also hold that special interest groups seeking to exercise influence by satisfying the candidates' need for campaign funds threaten the integrity of the election and governmental

1

processes. Compared with some other categories of spending, however, the amounts expended for political campaigns are low. The amount spent in 1987–1988 is about the same as the nation's two leading commercial advertisers—Philip Morris and Procter and Gamble—spent in 1987 to proclaim the quality of their products.[1] It represents a mere fraction of 1 percent of the $1.9 trillion spent in 1988 by federal, state, and local governments. And it is just a small portion of what is spent on cosmetics or gambling.

As with many other types of spending, there is no universally accepted criterion by which to determine when political spending becomes excessive. And no candidate wants to lose for having spent too little. Many factors have contributed to what sometimes appear to be high political campaign costs. During the course of the last two decades, campaigning at most levels has become a highly professionalized undertaking, involving the employment of pollsters, media specialists, computer specialists, fund-raising consultants, and a host of other campaign experts whose services are expensive and, in the estimation of many candidates and committees, essential. In addition, laws enacted at federal, state, and local levels to bring about disclosure of campaign finances and, in some cases, to impose limits on political contributions and expenditures have required candidates to hire election lawyers and political accountants to ensure compliance. Candidates and political committees must compete for attention not only with each other but also with commercial advertisers possessed of large budgets and able to advertise regularly—not just during a concentrated season. Finally, the Supreme Court has ruled that limits on campaign spending are unconstitutional except when imposed on candidates as a condition of accepting public funding. It has ruled further that even when campaigns are publicly funded, no limits may be placed on independent expenditures by individuals and committees that advocate any candidate's election or defeat.

CATEGORIES OF POLITICAL SPENDING, 1988

The political campaign spending bill of $2.7 billion in the 1987–1988 election cycle may be classified in eight major categories (see Table 1.1).

1. $500 million on presidential campaigns, including spending on prenomination campaigns that began as early as 1986;[2] spending by nominating convention committees; spending by major party, minor party, and independent presidential general election cam-

TABLE 1.1
The Campaign Spending Dollar in 1988 (in millions)

Presidential[a]	$ 500.0
Congressional[b]	457.7
National party[c]	328.3
Nonparty[d]	224.0
State and local party (nonpresidential, federal)[e]	87.5
State (nonfederal)[f]	540.0
Local (nonfederal)[g]	365.0
Ballot issues[h]	225.0
Total	$2,727.5

[a] Includes all presidential election–related spending in prenomination, convention, and general election periods.
[b] Includes all spending by congressional candidates.
[c] Includes all spending by national political party committees except money contributed to presidential and congressional candidates, coordinated expenditures on behalf of presidential candidates, and that portion of money spent on media advertising intended to influence presidential elections.
[d] Includes all spending reported by federally registered, nonparty political committees and their sponsors except money contributed to federal candidates and political party committees and money spent independently on behalf of presidential candidates. Also includes an estimated $150 million in political action committee administration and fund-raising costs paid by PAC sponsors but not reported to the FEC.
[e] Includes all spending reported by federally registered state and local party committees minus money contributed to or spent on behalf of presidential candidates, money contributed directly to congressional candidates, and estimated expenditures on grass-roots activities to support presidential tickets.
[f] Includes all spending by or on behalf of candidates for state-level political offices.
[g] Includes all spending by or on behalf of candidates for local offices.
[h] Includes all spending in campaigns to support or oppose state and local ballot issues.

Source: Citizens' Research Foundation.

paigns; and spending by national party committees on behalf of their presidential nominees. There were 330 presidential candidates filed with the Federal Election Commission (FEC), though most did not spend any money. Some 17 were on the general election ballot somewhere; along with the George Bush–Dan Quayle and the Michael Dukakis–Lloyd Bentsen tickets, only Lenora Fulani of the New Alliance party qualified on the November ballot in all fifty states.[3]

2. $457.7 million on congressional prenomination and general election campaigns, including money contributed directly to congressional candidates by party and nonparty political committees.[4]

3. $328.3 million of spending by national political party committees on administration, fund-raising, and other costs, excluding expenditures on behalf of presidential candidates and direct contributions to congressional candidates.
4. $224 million of spending by nonparty political committees and their sponsors, including an estimated $150 million in political action committee (PAC) administration and fund-raising costs paid by PAC sponsors but not reported to the FEC and excluding funds contributed directly to federal candidates or spent independently to influence presidential or congressional election results.
5. $87.5 million in spending by federally registered state and local party committees, excluding money contributed to or spent on behalf of presidential candidates and money contributed directly to congressional candidates.
6. $540 million in spending on state election campaigns to nominate and elect governors, state legislators, and other state government officials.
7. $365 million in spending on local election campaigns to nominate and elect county and municipal officials.
8. $225 million in spending on campaigns supporting or opposing state and local ballot propositions;[5] there were some 230 statewide proposals in forty-one states in 1988. In California alone, $139.8 million were spent on statewide ballot issues in the primary and general election campaigns.

From 1952 (the first year for which total political costs in the United States were calculated) to 1988, the progression in spending has shown steady increases in the presidential election cycles.[6]

1952	$ 140,000,000
1956	155,000,000
1960	175,000,000
1964	200,000,000
1968	300,000,000
1972	425,000,000
1976	540,000,000
1980	1,200,000,000
1984	1,800,000,000
1988	2,700,000,000

The increases over the years reflect not only inflation, higher levels of competition, the professionalization of politics, and more applications of high technology to politics but also the greater availability of comprehensive data due to improved laws requiring better public disclosure of political receipts and expenditures. The latter enables the researcher to tabulate more accurate totals of political spending at all levels.

PATTERNS IN POLITICAL GIVING

Although the costs of television and the total costs of campaigning have risen dramatically over recent decades, the percentage of those who donate to candidates and parties has not changed much since 1956. An overview of response to public opinion surveys from 1952 to 1988 is given in Table 1.2. Although these figures are subject to a polling error of up to 4 percent, their replication over the years gives confidence that the upper and lower parameters of giving are accurate.

The surveys show a rather steady increase in the number of contributors in the 1950s through 1968, when the number dropped. The number rose again in 1972, only to drop once more in the post-Watergate period. Moreover, survey findings spanning more than four decades indicate that a reservoir of untapped potential for campaign funds continues to exist. Throughout the 1940s and 1950s, the Gallup Poll asked individuals if they would be willing to make political contributions; approximately one-third of those surveyed said they would. In the 1960s, this figure rose to 40 percent. And a June 1981 Gallup Poll found that 39 percent of respondents expressed a desire to join one or more special interest groups.[7]

From 1952 to 1988, between 4 and 13 percent of the total adult population said they contributed to politics at some level in presidential election years. Clearly, some persons contribute in more than one category.

One recent study of patterns of giving concludes that

While it is true that more and more people are now asked, by phone and mail, to make political contributions, the response rate is generally very low. Modern technology notwithstanding, face-to-face appeals continue to be the most effective way of soliciting political contributions. There does not seem to be a large, undifferentiated electorate just waiting for an invitation to contribute to campaigns.[8]

Table 1.2 seems to bear out this conclusion.

One relevant factor present in the years 1972 to 1984 was missing in 1988: A federal income tax credit for portions of political contributions was repealed by the Tax Reform Act of 1986.[9] Whatever incentive the tax benefit may have given contributors previously was not available in 1988.

TABLE 1.2
Percentage of National Adult Population Making Political Contributions,
1952–1988

| Year | Polling Organization | Contributed To | | Total[a] |
		Republican	Democrat	
1952	SRC	3	1	4
1956	Gallup	3	6	9
1956	SRC	5	5	10
1960	Gallup	4	4	9
1960	Gallup			12
1960	SRC	7	4	11
1964	Gallup	6	4	12
1964	SRC	6	4	11
1968	SRC	4	4	9[b]
1972	SRC	4	5	10[c]
1974	SRC	3	3	8[d]
1976	Gallup	3	3	8[e]
1976	SRC	4	4	9[f]
1980	CPS[g]	7	3	13.4[h]
1984	CPS	5	4	12.5[i]
1988	CPS	4	3	7.2[j]

[a] The total percentage may add up to a total different from the total of Democrat and Republican contributions because of individuals contributing to both major parties, nonparty groups, or combinations of these.

[b] Includes 0.7 percent who contributed to Wallace's American Independent party (AIP).

[c] Includes contributors to the American Independent party.

[d] Includes 0.7 percent who contributed to both parties and 0.8 percent who contributed to minor parties.

[e] Includes 1 percent to another party and 1 percent to Do Not Know or No Answer.

[f] Republican and Democratic figures are rounded. The total includes 0.6 percent who gave to both parties, 0.4 percent to other, and 0.3 percent Do Not Know.

[g] The Center for Political Studies (CPS), located at the University of Michigan, is the successor to the Survey Research Center (SRC).

[h] Includes persons who gave to special interest groups. Because some 6.8 percent of those surveyed fell into this category, it appears that many contributed in two or all three categories.

[i] Includes persons giving to groups supporting and opposing ballot propositions and candidates.

[j] Includes 0.5 percent who gave to both parties or to candidates from both parties.

Source: Survey Research Center, University of Michigan: data direct from center or from Angus Campbell, Philip E. Converse, and Donald E. Stokes, *The American Voter* (New York: John Wiley and Sons, 1960), p. 91; 1980 data from Ruth S. Jones and Warren E. Miller, "Financing Campaigns: Macro Level Innovation and Micro Level Response," *Western Political Quarterly,* vol. 38, no. 2, 1987, pp. 187–210; 1984 data from Ruth S. Jones, "Campaign Contributions and Campaign Solicitations: 1984" (Paper presented at the meeting of the Southern Political Science Association, Nashville, Tennessee, November 6–9, 1985); Gallup data direct or from Roper Opinion Research Center, Williams College, and from the American Institute of Political Opinion (Gallup Poll).

NOTES

1. R. Craig Endicott, "Philip Morris Unseats P & G as Top Advertising Spender," *Advertising Age,* September 28, 1988, p. 1.

2. "Presidential Prenomination Campaigns," *Report on Financial Activity, 1987–1988,* Federal Election Commission, Washington, D.C., 1989, p. 10.

3. "The Other Choices for President," *Congressional Quarterly Weekly Report,* vol. 46, no. 45, November 5, 1988, p. 3184.

4. "$458 Million Spent by 1988 Congressional Campaigns," Federal Election Commission, press release, February 24, 1989, pp. 1–67.

5. Estimate for 1987–1988 based on "Campaign Spending 1988: IRC Study," *Initiative & Referendum: The Power of the People,* Initiative Resource Center, Spring 1989, pp. 6–7; and "Campaign Spending Records Set by Three November Ballot Measures," California Fair Political Practices Commission, Sacramento, Calif., press release, March 30, 1989, pp. 1–13.

6. See Herbert E. Alexander and Brian A. Haggerty, *Financing the 1984 Election* (Lexington, Mass.: Lexington Books, 1987), p. 127, fn. 1.

7. Gallup Poll, "Participation in Interest Groups High," *Gallup Report,* August 1981, p. 45.

8. Ruth S. Jones, "Contributing as Participation," in Margaret Latus Nugent and John R. Johannes, eds., *Money, Elections, and Democracy: Reforming Congressional Campaign Finance* (Boulder, Colo.: Westview Press, 1990), p. 40.

9. Public Law 99-513, 100 Stat. 2082 (October 21, 1986).

2

FINANCING THE
PRESIDENTIAL ELECTIONS:
SEEKING THE NOMINATIONS

In the 1970s, the laws regulating federal election campaign financing in the United States underwent dramatic changes. In regard to presidential campaigns, enactments including public funding, contribution and expenditure limits, and disclosure requirements were intended to minimize opportunities for undue financial influence on officeholders and to make the election process more open and competitive. The laws have accomplished some of their aims, but they also have had some unintended, and not always salutary, consequences. The degree to which the laws have failed to achieve their intended effects testifies at least as much to the inventiveness of political actors in circumventing the laws and to the intractability of election campaign finance in a pluralistic society as to the deficiencies of the laws themselves.

The Federal Election Campaign Act of 1971,[1] the Revenue Act of 1971,[2] and the FECA amendments of 1974,[3] 1976,[4] and 1979[5] thoroughly revised the rules of the game for political candidates, parties, and contributors. In regard to presidential campaigns, the laws provided for public matching funds for qualified candidates in the prenomination period, public treasury grants to pay the costs of the two major parties' national nominating conventions, and public treasury grants for the

8

major party general election candidates. They also established criteria whereby minor parties and new parties and their candidates can qualify for public funds to pay nominating convention and general election campaign costs.

The public funds, earmarked through a federal income tax checkoff, were intended to help provide or to supply in entirety the money serious candidates need to present themselves and their ideas to the electorate. In the prenomination period, public funding was intended to make the nomination process more competitive and to encourage candidates to broaden their bases of support by seeking out large numbers of relatively small contributions matchable with public funds. In the general election period, flat grants to major party candidates were intended to provide the basic money needed soon after the nominating conventions, to be supplemented by national party coordinated expenditures on behalf of the presidential ticket.

Contribution and expenditure limits also were enacted, although the Supreme Court subsequently ruled that spending limits are permissible only in publicly financed campaigns.[6] These laws were intended to control large donations with their potential for corruption, to minimize financial disparities among candidates, and to reduce opportunities for abuse. Finally, laws requiring full and timely disclosure of campaign receipts and expenditures were put in place to help the electorate make informed choices among candidates and to make it possible to monitor compliance with the campaign finance laws by establishing the Federal Election Commission.

THE REGULATORY FRAMEWORK

Candidates who seek presidential nomination do not enjoy unrestricted access to the electorate. Interposed between the candidates and potential voters is the government, acting through campaign finance and political broadcast regulations intended to ensure that candidates compete, as much as possible, on a fair and equitable basis. Political parties at both national and state levels also intervene in the process of communications between candidates and voters through the rules and procedures the parties adopt regulating the methods and timing of delegate selection. Laws, rules, and procedures, then, circumscribe the candidates' campaign activities. At the same time, they are the object of much probing and testing by candidates seeking advantage over their opponents while still remaining within the bounds established by government and party.

The basic laws that governed fund-raising, spending, and reporting the use of campaign money in the 1988 prenomination campaigns were the same as those that had been in effect four years earlier, and in fact they had changed little since they were first applied in the 1976 campaigns. Under these laws, candidates for the presidential nomination in 1988 could accept no more than $1,000 from any individual contributor and no more than $5,000 from any multicandidate committee (PAC). The candidates were allowed to contribute an unlimited amount to their own campaigns, unless they accepted public funding. In that case, they were permitted to contribute a maximum of $50,000 in personal or family funds. No candidate was allowed to accept a contribution from a prohibited source, including corporate and labor union treasury funds, or cash contributions in excess of $100.

Public matching funds were available for candidates who raised $5,000 in each of twenty states, in contributions from individuals of $250 or less. Donations from PACs were not eligible for matching funds. The federal government matched each contribution to qualified candidates from individuals up to $250 per contributor, but the total federal subsidy to any candidate could not exceed $11.6 million, one-half the prenomination campaign spending limit. The matching funds were drawn from the Presidential Election Campaign Fund, established by the Revenue Act of 1971. Under that law, taxpayers were permitted to use a checkoff procedure on their federal income tax forms to earmark a small portion of their tax liabilities—$1 for individuals and $2 for married persons filing jointly—for the campaign fund to provide money for public funding of presidential election campaigns. Although the Federal Election Commission could not begin releasing matching funds to candidates until January 1, 1988, the candidates were permitted to begin collecting matchable contributions as early as January 1, 1987.

All candidates for presidential nomination in 1984 who accepted public matching funds could spend no more than $23.1 million, plus 20 percent—$4.6 million—for fund-raising. Unlike the contribution limits, which have remained at the level originally fixed by the 1974 FECA amendments, the expenditure limit is adjusted for inflation, using 1974 as the base year. As Table 2.3 indicates, the 1988 overall prenomination campaign spending limit represents a net increase of about $12.2 million compared with the 1976 limit and an increase of about $2.9 million compared with the 1984 limit. Candidates accepting matching funds also were bound by spending limits in the individual states. They were permitted to spend no more than the greater of $200,000 or sixteen cents per eligible voter, plus a cost-of-living increase using 1974 as the base year. Payments made by the candidates for legal and accounting services to comply with the campaign law were exempted from the law's spending limits, but the candidates were required to report such payments to the Federal Election Commission. Those who did not accept public funding were not bound by the overall or the individual state spending limits. All 15 major candidates for nomination, however, accepted public funds and accordingly were required to honor the spending limits.

Finally, all the candidates were required to submit regular reports to the FEC disclosing information about their campaign organizations' receipts and expenditures. The FEC, in turn, made these reports available to the public. The reports had to identify by name, address, occupation, and employer all contributors of more than $200; they also had to itemize each campaign expenditure of more than $200, indicating the name and address of the recipient and the purpose of the expenditure.

Four presidential elections have now been conducted under the FECA, its amendments, and its companion laws—a sufficient experience from which to draw some conclusions about the impact of the laws and to determine whether they have had their intended effects.[7] The costs to the voters, the taxpayers, and the candidates' campaigns have been considerable. An assessment is in order: How well did the public funding system for presidential campaigns and the accompanying expenditure limits serve the candidates and the American people?

THE 1988 PRESIDENTIAL COSTS

In the 1987–1988 election cycle, political candidates and committees at all levels—federal, state, and local—spent $2.7 billion on political campaigns. About 18.5 percent, or $500 million, was spent to elect a president. The spending in each phase was apportioned as indicated in Table 2.1. Drawing together all reported expenditures, some $233.5 million was spent by and on behalf of candidates seeking nomination (through June 30, 1989), $42.1 million related to the two major party conventions, and $208.3 million in the general election period. Miscellaneous spending accounted for the remainder of the $500 million total.

Although the 1988 spending was high, when seen in perspective in Table 2.2, the long-term trends are not so alarming. When adjusted for inflation since 1960, the costs of presidential campaigns have increased only by a factor of 4, whereas aggregate unadjusted costs have risen almost 17-fold from 1960–1988. The $500 million cost, however, represents a whopping 54 percent increase from the 1984 cost of $325 million.[8] With no incumbent running in 1988, the presidency was wide open for the first time in twenty years.

The intense competition for nomination in both parties resulted in a combined cost of about $212 million in candidate spending,[9] twice that of 1984, when no Republican challenged President Ronald Reagan's renomination but a competitive Democratic contest was waged. General

TABLE 2.1
Costs of Electing a President, 1988 (in millions)

Prenomination (as of June 30, 1989)		
Spending by major party candidates	$199.6	
Compliance[a]	12.4	
Independent expenditures	4.1	
Delegate candidate spending	.1	
Communication costs[b]	.2	
Labor spending	15.0	
Minor parties[c]	2.1	
Subtotal		$233.5
Conventions (including host cities and committees)		
Republicans	18.0	
Democrats	22.4	
Subtotal		$ 40.4
General election		
Spending by major party candidates[d]	92.2	
Compliance	6.1	
Parties[e]	61.6	
Republican National Committee media[f]	5.8	
Independent expenditures[g]	10.1	
Communication costs	2.0	
Labor, corporate, association spending	27.5	
Minor parties[h]	3.0	
Subtotal		$208.3
Miscellaneous expenses[i]	17.8	
Grand total		$500.0

[a] Not available for Jack Kemp, whose compliance costs were not specified in his reports.

[b] Prenomination independent expenditures and communication costs are through July 15 for Republicans, August 15 for Democrats.

[c] Reported for prenomination campaign by Lenora B. Fulani.

[d] Includes $46.1 million in public funds spent by each major party candidate.

[e] Includes $43 million in "soft money" expenditures related to presidential campaigns and convention activities.

[f] According to the 1988 Chairman's Report, the RNC spent $11.5 million on a national media advertising campaign; one-half its value was assigned to the presidential campaign.

[g] Negative advertising made up $2.9 million of the total.

[h] Includes $1,327,926 spent by Ron Paul, the Libertarian party candidate; $1,053,221 spent by Lyndon LaRouche of LaRouche '88; $465,943 by Lenora B. Fulani, the New Alliance party candidate; and other minor party and independent candidates.

[i] Includes that portion of presidential PAC spending in 1985–1988 used to fund candidates' preannouncement activities; a reasonable portion of funds spent by nonpartisan organizations to conduct voter registration and turnout drives that benefited specific presidential candidates; costs for advertising and communications by various organizations on issues closely related to presidential campaigns; and miscellaneous out-of-pocket expenses.

Source: Citizens' Research Foundation.

TABLE 2.2
Presidential Spending, 1960–1988 (adjusted for inflation, 1960 = 100)

Year	Actual Spending[a]	CPI (1960 Base)	Adjusted Spending[a]
1960	30.0	100.0	30.0
1964	60.0	104.7	57.3
1968	100.0	117.5	85.1
1972	138.0	141.2	97.7
1976	160.0	192.2	83.2
1980	275.0	278.1	98.9
1984	325.0	346.8	93.7
1988	500.0	385.4	126.5

[a]All spending figures are in millions and include prenomination, convention, and general election costs.

Source: Citizens' Research Foundation.

election spending rose over 1984 mainly because of the infusion of large amounts of soft money raised and spent in each major party campaign. Inflation and entitlements for eligible parties to hold the 1988 conventions and for candidates in the prenomination and general election phases began to eat up the balances of the Presidential Election Campaign Fund, supplied by dwindling income tax checkoffs. Clearly, the U.S. system of public funding is approaching jeopardy, and 1988 demonstrated many problems that need correction.

Efforts in 1987 and 1988 to extend public financing to Senate and House campaigns diverted attention from the fine-tuning that was desirable in the laws governing presidential campaigns. There has been no change in federal election law since 1979, but most of the presidential election provisions have not been altered since 1974. There is one exception, however: Amounts of public financing and expenditure limits were adjusted to changes in the Consumer Price Index—but not enough to keep pace with the escalation of campaign costs at a much higher rate than inflation. Table 2.3 demonstrates the amounts of public funding and expenditure limits as adjusted from 1976 to 1988.

The problems in 1988 have spurred both increased public concern and the attention of President Bush and the 101st Congress. On June 29, 1989, the president proposed to Congress a series of election reforms;[10] there were also scores of legislative bills introduced in the Congress. An evaluation of how well or poorly the election law operated in 1988 will help focus policymakers on trouble areas requiring revision in the Federal Election Campaign Act as it relates to presidential campaigns.

TABLE 2.3
Major Party Presidential Campaign Expenditure Limits and Public Funding,
1976–1988 (in millions)

	Prenomination Campaign				General Election Campaign		
						National	
	National	Exempt	Overall		Public	Party	Overall
	Spending	Fund-	Spending	Nominating	Treasury	Spending	Spending
Year	Limit[a]	Raising[b]	Limit[c]	Convention	Grant[d]	Limit[e]	Limit[f]
1976	$10.9	+ $2.2	= $13.1	$2.2[g]	$21.8	+ $3.2	= $25.0
1980	14.7	+ 2.9	= 17.7	4.4	29.4	+ 4.6	= 34.0
1984	20.2	+ 4.0	= 24.2	8.1	40.4	+ 6.9	= 47.3
1988	23.1	+ 4.6	= 27.7	9.2	46.1	+ 8.3	= 54.4

[a] Based on $10 million plus cost-of-living increases (COLA) using 1974 as the base year. Eligible candidates may receive no more than one-half the national spending limit in public matching funds. To become eligible, candidates must raise $5,000 in private contributions of $250 or less in each of twenty states. The federal government matches each contribution to qualified candidates up to $250. Publicly funded candidates also must observe spending limits in the individual states equal to the greater of $200,000 + COLA (base year 1974), or $.16 × the voting-age population (VAP) of the state + COLA.
[b] Candidates may spend up to 20 percent of the national spending limit for fund-raising.
[c] Legal and accounting expenses to ensure compliance with the law are exempt from the spending limit.
[d] Based on $20 million + COLA (base year 1974).
[e] Based on $.02 × VAP of the United States + COLA.
[f] Compliance costs are exempt from the spending limit.
[g] Based on $2 million + COLA (base year 1974). Under the 1979 FECA amendments, the basic grant was raised to $3 million. In 1984, Congress raised the basic grant to $4 million.

Source: Citizens' Research Foundation, based on FEC data.

PRECANDIDACY PACs AND THE 1988 ELECTIONS

Once a person declares his or her intention to run as a candidate for the presidency and registers a principal campaign committee with the Federal Election Commission, the meter begins to run on expenditure limitations. One way of circumventing these limits is to remain an undeclared candidate for as long as possible and to have a Political Action Committee (PAC) to support precandidacy political activity. Ronald Reagan was the first to use such a personal PAC to fund efforts he made after his 1976 prenomination defeat, thereby laying the groundwork for a 1980 candidacy. Reagan's PAC, Citizens for the Republic, was partly funded by the $1.6 million left over from his 1976 campaign. Although the PAC was described as a way to help conservatives at the state and local party levels, in fact "most of the PAC's funds were used to hire staff and consultants, develop fund-raising programs, recruit volunteers, subsidize Reagan's travel and public appearances, and host receptions on his behalf."[11] Only 10 percent of the $6.3 million he raised was contributed to candidates for federal office.

According to political scientist Anthony Corrado, precandidacy PACs have, since 1980, become "one of the biggest loopholes in the federal campaign-finance system."[12] An overview of presidential PAC spending for the years 1980, 1984, and 1988 is shown in Table 2.4. Such spending for 1988 was more than twice the combined amounts spent in advance of the 1980 and 1984 elections.

The largest proliferation of such precandidacy PACs took place in the months leading up to the 1988 campaign. Some $25.2 million was spent by PACs standing behind an undeclared candidate for the presidential nomination, as shown in Table 2.5. In the first open presidential contest since 1968, 9 of the eventual 14 declared major party candidates for president exercised their option to begin their efforts with a PAC. The PACs of candidates Bush, Robert Dole, and Jack Kemp accounted for 85 percent of the total amounts spent in the 1988 election cycle. Democratic candidates spent less than $2 million, and Dukakis did not have a presidential PAC.[13]

The Federal Election Campaign Act requires full disclosure of moneys, limits individual contributions to $1,000 for presidential candidates accepting matching funds, and mandates a limit on expenditures for both the nomination contests and the general election. In contrast, the precandidacy PACs allow undeclared candidates to accept contributions of up to $5,000 a year for each year they keep the PAC active. In

TABLE 2.4
Adjusted Expenditures of Candidate-Sponsored PACs, 1980–1988 (in millions)

Election Cycle	Actual Spending[a]	Adjusted Spending[a]	No. of PACs	Adjusted Average Spending/Committee[a]
1980	$ 7.5	$ 6.4	4	$1.6
1984	7.0	4.1	5	.8
1988	25.2	13.0	9	1.4

[a]Figures in 1976 dollars. Amounts noted are based on the total expenditures by these committees adjusted on a per annum basis for increases in the consumer price index with 1976 as the base year (1976=100). Adjusted expenditures for 1988 calculated on the basis of the unadjusted consumer price index (1967=100) for June 1988.

Source: Adapted from Anthony J. Corrado, "Honored in the Breach: Candidate PACs and the Post-Reform Presidential Selection Process" (Ph.D. diss., Boston College, 1990), p. 143. Reprinted with permission.

TABLE 2.5
Expenditures of Candidate-Sponsored PACs, 1988 Election Cycle (in thousands)

Name of PAC	1985	1986	1987	1988[a]	Total
Americans for the National Interest (Babbitt)	45.7	110.7	0.0	0.0	156.3
Campaign America (Dole)	390.4	2,859.1	2,917.0	378.3	6,544.8
Campaign for Prosperity (Kemp)	1,198.9	2,048.8	679.6	233.7	4,161.0
Committee for America (Haig)	0.0	599.7	465.3	10.0	1,075.0
Committee for Freedom (Robertson)	56.3	514.6	67.5	45.8	684.2
The Democracy Fund (Simon)	135.2	278.4	37.5	14.5	465.6
Effective Government Committee (Gephardt)	317.7	750.5	102.1	53.4	1,223.7
Fund for America's Future (Bush)	1,545.9	7,656.6	1,291.6	287.6	10,787.7
Fund for '86 (Biden)	0.0	121.2	12.0	0.0	133.2
Annual Total	3,690.1	14,939.5	5,572.6	1,023.3	25,225.5

[a]Amounts reported through June 30, 1988.

Source: Data based on expenditures reported by each committee in Federal Election Commission, Committee Index of Disclosure Documents (C Index), 1985–1988, computer printouts, n.d. Adapted from Anthony J. Corrado, "Honored in the Breach: Candidate PACs and the Post-Reform Presidential Selection Process" (Ph.D. diss., Boston College, 1990), p. 143. Reprinted with permission.

addition, once the candidacy is declared, that same contributor can give the maximum amount—only $1,000—to the newly formed campaign committee. An additional advantage is the lack of spending limits on PACs, allowing undeclared candidates to spend as much as they want without having such spending count toward their expenditure limits.

An example cited by Corrado is George Bush's Fund for America's Future. This PAC was set up on April 25, 1985, supposedly to help other Republican efforts. However, of the $11.2 million raised, it spent just $844,000 in support of other federal candidates. What the PAC enabled then Vice President Bush to do was to "hire a national staff of 50 persons . . . hire political organizers in Iowa, New Hampshire, and Michigan . . . develop direct mail fund-raising programs, prepare policy papers, and conduct polls. . . . Yet none of its expenditures was applicable to the Bush campaign's spending."[14]

The presidential PAC amounts do not include funds spent by the exploratory committee of Congresswoman Patricia Schroeder (D–CO) because she declined to become an announced candidate for the presidency. After Gary Hart left the race, leaving the Democrats with no clear front-runner, Schroeder announced the formation of the Schroeder Fund for the Future. Using the fund as a springboard, she began a series of appearances meant to test the waters for a possible presidential bid. After raising just $800,000 of the $2 million goal she had set for herself to finance a viable campaign for the nomination, Schroeder announced her withdrawal from a race she had never officially entered. In 1990, the FEC ruled that she could only transfer $1,000 from the fund to her congressional campaign committee. In a discussion that centered on the hybrid nature of such a PAC, the FEC concluded that it was "more akin to an unaffiliated, issue-oriented organization" because contributions made to the fund were not contributed "to help elect an officially declared candidate."[15]

PRENOMINATION CAMPAIGNS

The major problem manifested in the 1988 prenomination phase of the presidential selection process was the inflexibility of the law in responding to highly competitive campaigns in both parties and to events such as Super Tuesday. March 8 was almost half of a national primary—twenty states for the Democrats and seventeen for the Republicans. The candidates therefore had to be selective in marshaling and allocating their resources so that they would not be too short for the rest of the long presidential season. Thus, candidates could not spend the $5 million minimum that most experts said was necessary to campaign effectively in that many states or to purchase spot announcements in the fifty or more media markets involved.

If Bob Dole or Pat Robertson had remained competitive with George Bush through the California primary and up to the time of the Republican National Convention, the leading spenders would have been unable to pay out much money in ensuing primaries and caucuses without exceeding the overall expenditure limit that the law imposed—$23.1 million plus a 20 percent overage of $4.6 million for fund-raising costs, totaling $27.7 million per candidate. Even without such competition, Bush had to curtail his schedule a month before the convention in order to conserve his spending sufficiently to avoid violating the election law.[16] In contrast, Dukakis's main opposition in seeking the Democratic nomination was Jesse Jackson, whose middling spending did not push him toward the upper limits as the Bush, Dole, and Robertson competition had raised the ante for the Republicans.

Within the $27.7 million total limitations, as shown in Table 2.3, are sublimits in each state based on population size.[17] These restrictions on how much a candidate can spend in each state have become wholly unrealistic in this day of media-dominated, regional presidential campaigning. They have also forced candidates to engage in subterfuges that make a mockery of the law and further confuse the funding picture.

Consider the psychological stake of winning in the first two contests: in Iowa, where the spending limit was $775,217, and in New Hampshire, where the limit was $461,000. Candidates found ways to assign spending to their national headquarters, to surrounding states, or to fund-raising costs, a separate accounting procedure. For example, autos were rented in Massachusetts for use in New Hampshire and credited against the larger Massachusetts limit. The Federal Election Commission permitted 80 percent of the television time purchased on Boston stations (reaching 80 percent of the New Hampshire population) to be allocated to the Massachusetts limit, where the primary was not held until Super Tuesday. Richard Gephardt put tag-end requests for contributions on his television ads and allocated half the costs to fund-raising; thus, the expenditures were not credited against the New Hampshire limits. By sanctioning such allocations, the FEC allowed the candidates to avoid exceeding the state limits.[18] And in any case, documented excessive spending only brings a FEC fine in the amount of the overspending, months after the event, and it is considered by pragmatic candidates as a cost of "doing business." As L. Sandy Maisel has written, "Certainly the intent of the law was not to create incentives for candidates to cheat on the state-by-state limits, because the consequences of being caught cheating were less serious for a campaign than the consequences of losing a caucus or primary."[19]

The ultimate absurdity of the state limits, however, can be found by adding them all up. For the fifty states, this produced a total of $70 million, almost three times the $27.7 million national limit (including fund-raising costs) that candidates could legally spend.

In the 1988 prenomination campaigns, the major party candidates spent $212 million; matching funds, as shown in Table 2.6, amounted to $67.2 million, accounting for 31 percent;[20] thus, the United States government was the largest single contributor. A summary of matching fund activity for each candidate, including numbers of contributors and amounts certified, is shown in Table 2.7.

In addition, independent expenditures were $3.5 million for all candidates ($3 million of which was spent on behalf of George Bush), and $656,179 was used in negative campaigning in opposition to various candidates. Independent expenditures on behalf of Democratic candidates totaled only $81,681, but the negative spending in opposition to Democratic candidates was $638,637, including $395,974 against front-runner Michael Dukakis and $163,755 against Jesse Jackson. A more extensive discussion of presidential independent expenditure is found in Chapter 4 and in Table 4.1. Other related expenditures, such

TABLE 2.6
Payouts from the Presidential Election Campaign Fund, 1988

Prenomination		
Republicans	$ 35,496,466	
Democrats	30,767,102	
National Alliance	938,798	
Subtotal		$ 67,202,367
Conventions		
Democrats	$ 9,220,000	
Republicans	9,220,000	
Subtotal		$ 18,440,000
General Election		
Bush-Quayle	$ 46,100,000	
Dukakis-Bentsen	46,100,000	
Subtotal		$ 92,200,000
Total paid out		$177,842,367

Source: Federal Election Commission, as of July 19, 1989.

TABLE 2.7
Summary of Matching Fund Activity for 1988 Presidential Prenomination Candidates

Candidate	Number of Submissions	Amount Requested	Number of Contributions	Number of Resubmissions	Amount Certified by FEC
Babbitt	14	$ 1,096,604	9,088	0	$ 1,078,939
Biden	0	0	0	0	0
Dukakis	11	9,203,082	91,210	0	9,040,027
Gephardt	19	3,975,487	49,944	0	3,108,350
Gore	13	3,917,985	39,984	0	3,853,402
Hart	2	1,136,687	14,164	0	1,122,282
Jackson	19	9,180,588	214,208	0	8,021,707
LaRouche	7	829,521	6,393	0	825,577
Simon	16	3,979,256	67,431	2	3,706,106
Bush	13	8,587,743	101,694	0	8,393,099
Dole	15	7,942,585	119,352	0	7,618,116
du Pont	8	2,636,385	42,187	0	2,550,954
Haig	8	567,199	3,452	0	538,539
Kemp	21	6,154,333	192,077	2	5,984,774
Robertson	16	11,282,764	238,581	0	10,410,987
Fulani	12	963,740	55,736	0	938,798
Totals	194	$71,453,959	1,245,501	4	$67,150,698

Source: FEC Reports on Financial Activity, 1987–1988: Final Report, "Presidential Prenomination Campaigns," August 1989, p. 7.

as those by labor unions in parallel campaigning, were shown earlier in Table 2.1.

George Bush and Michael Dukakis had two common characteristics: They had the most money early, and they had sufficient funds to sustain their campaigns throughout.[21] Bush's successes were more related to his status as vice president, to his impressive résumé, and to the political obligations people owed to him than to his spending; he won decisively on Super Tuesday despite being outspent in twelve states.[22]

Dukakis had a decided advantage in early fund-raising. For example, by the end of 1987, he had raised more than twice as much as his closest competitor in financial terms, Richard Gephardt. Dukakis's financial advantage enabled him to sustain his campaign through some rocky outcomes in Iowa and elsewhere. As of December 31, 1987, the Democratic candidates' fund-raising totals, in rounded amounts, were as follows:

Dukakis	$10.6 million
Gephardt	4.4 million
Gore	3.8 million
Simon	3.8 million
Hart	2.0 million
Jackson	2.0 million
Babbitt	2.0 million

Bush had a similar early advantage in fund-raising, made manifest by the ease with which a sitting vice president was able to raise large numbers of the maximum $1,000 contributions. The Republican candidates' fund-raising totals as of December 31, 1987, in rounded amounts, were:

Bush	$18.7 million
Dole	14.0 million
Robertson	14.0 million
Kemp	7.5 million
du Pont	4.5 million
Haig	1.5 million

Bush overspent in 1987 on a large and expensive organization, requiring him to conserve carefully during 1988, and, as noted, he curtailed his campaigning in the spring to avoid violating the overall expenditure limitation.

A number of candidates borrowed money in late 1987 against anticipated matching funds that were not available until early January 1988. In addition, by the end of 1987, Patricia Schroeder, Joseph Biden,

Paul Laxalt, and Gary Hart had withdrawn from the contest. Hart, as will be noted, reentered and exited a second time in March 1988. Excluding Hart, who is listed below, these candidates had raised more than $5 million.

The Dukakis Campaign

The Dukakis campaign provided significant data on its receipts, summarized below:

Sources of funds:	(in millions)
Non-direct mail	$17.0
Direct mail	2.4
Raised	$19.4
Transfer from Massachusetts gubernatorial surplus	.4
	$19.8
Matching funds	9.0
Legal and accounting funds	2.5
Total raised for Dukakis for President	$31.3

Regional receipts	(in millions)
New England	$ 7.9
Mid-Atlantic	5.7
South	1.9
Midwest	1.2
West	2.7

Top 10 states	
1. Massachusetts	$7,044,251
2. New York	3,012,645
3. California	2,282,128
4. New Jersey	965,226
5. Florida	715,094
6. Ohio	522,222
7. Connecticut	454,488
8. Washington, D.C.	440,171
9. Illinois	415,482
10. Pennsylvania	393,111

Information about the financing of Dukakis's successful campaign for nomination is revealing. The regional receipts showed a strong eastern bias, with the exception of California, which provided $2.3 million in contributions. In all, 114,000 contributions were counted, and the average was $171. Dukakis about matched Dole by collecting 7,184 individual contributions of $1,000 each. Kitty Dukakis, the candidate's wife, was credited with raising $500,000 at events where she spoke. Some 1,046 finance committee members raised at least $10,000 each, and 203 members of the board of directors were credited with fulfilling commitments to raise at least $25,000 each.

Direct mail efforts in the Dukakis campaign raised $2.4 million, with a 3.5 percent response rate on repeats on the house list (composed of individuals who contributed earlier) and a 1.5 percent response rate on lists prospecting new contributors. The net mail receipts, after costs, were $1.6 million, but with matching funds, they amounted to $3.4 million. Thus, matching funds give incentive to such fund-raising in campaigns where direct mail is productive.

Michael Dukakis directed that no PAC contributions be accepted for his campaign. However, his campaign made maximum use of corporate top managers who raised money from their colleagues in major corporations, particularly those in high-tech companies in Massachusetts and on Wall Street, where Dukakis had close ties.[23] Thus, his campaign was able to get 10 or 20 contributions in amounts of $1,000 each from corporate executives; PAC contributions would have been limited to $5,000 for each corporation.

Dukakis prenomination campaign expenditures follow:

Headquarters	$12,344,807
States	5,689,298
Scheduling/travel	4,347,183
Media production	1,463,085
Media placement	3,796,914
Polling	428,620
Total	$28,069,907

For a campaign that participated in almost every primary and caucus, the figures reveal relatively high national headquarters expenditures in relation to state campaigns and very high media production costs in relation to airtime costs.

The Gephardt Campaign

Richard Gephardt received $6,968,822 in contributions, about one-third in amounts of $1,000 or more and about one-half in amounts of $250–$999. The $1,000-or-more category included $617,065 contributed by PACs. Gephardt personally contributed $50,000 to his own campaign.

The Bush Campaign

The Bush campaign raised and spent the full amounts permissible under federal law. Its receipts included three notable sources: $2,000 from the candidate and his wife; $670,567 from PACs; and $16,500,000 from 16,500 contributors, in the amount of $1,000 each. Fund-raising cost twenty-one cents per dollar raised, and an additional $3.7 million was raised to cover compliance costs.

Media expenditures for Bush indicate that $3,197,696 was spent to purchase television time, and $239,620 was used to purchase radio time. (Production costs are not available.) Of these amounts, combined television and radio spending in Iowa amounted to $142,443; in New Hampshire, they were $213,070.[24]

The Dole Campaign

In contrast, the Dole campaign raised 7,500 individual contributions of $1,000 each—considerably less than Bush in that category—but raised $848,931 in PAC contributions, some $180,000 more than Bush received from that source.

The Kemp Campaign

The Kemp campaign provided complete information on its receipts and expenditures from December 1, 1986, through July 31, 1988. The overview follows:

Sources of funds:			
Direct mail	$ 5,677,100		
Fund-raising events	3,076,500		
National finance committee	625,800		
Personal solicitations	589,700		
Miscellaneous	357,100		
Gross contributions	$10,816,200		
Contribution refunds	(250,700)		
Net contributions		$10,565,500	
Matching funds		5,694,600	
Interest income		10,800	
Total funds raised			$16,270,900
Bank loans			3,570,000
Total sources of funds			$19,840,900
Uses of funds			
Operating expenditures	$16,328,200		
Refunds, rebates, etc.	(198,400)		
Net operating expenditures		$16,129,800	
Bank loan repayments		3,570,000	
Total uses of funds			$19,699,800
Total campaign surplus			$ 141,100

Of particular interest here are the extraordinary efforts in direct mail, bringing in more than half of the contributions and outperforming the competitive Bush and Dole receipts from that source. The following summary of Kemp's expenditures shows the high cost of the fund-raising effort—$6.2 million—a large part of it in direct mail costs. But as demonstrated in the Dukakis campaign, matching funds for small contributions can make direct mail productive. Not shown as a separate receipt entry is $64,998 in PAC contributions. The Kemp expenditures included:

Chairman's office	$ 232,600
National political	1,216,800
Midwest regional office	583,800
Michigan state office	210,600
Other state offices	526,800
New Hampshire state office	296,600
Scheduling and advance	299,900
Candidate support	1,183,200
Surrogate tours	37,700
Speechwriting and polling	194,400
Advertising	2,290,900
Communications	240,900
Administration	1,165,400
Fund-raising	6,229,000
Treasurer's office	1,122,000
Close-down operations	497,600
Total operating expenditures	$16,328,200

Self-Contributions/Loans

The Federal Election Commission has provided information about prenomination candidates' self-contributions and loans to their own campaigns, as follows:[25]

Candidate contributions to own campaigns	
Babbitt	$41,000
Gephardt	50,000
Bush	2,000
du Pont	50,000
Candidate loans to own campaigns	
Gore	$40,000 (repaid)
Simon	45,000
Haig	50,000
Robertson	25,000 (repaid)

Under federal law, presidential candidates who accept public financing are limited in the amount—$50,000—they and their immediate families can contribute to their own campaigns. Two candidates made such contributions in the full amount; two made substantial personal contributions—Babbitt nearing the limit with $41,000 and Bush with $2,000—and four others lent varying amounts to their campaigns.

PAC Contributions

The FEC also tabulated data on PAC contributions, as shown in Table 2.8. Notably, Robert Dole, who remained U.S. Senate minority leader during his presidential campaign, received the highest amount of PAC contributions—even more than Bush, who received the nomination. In all, PAC contributions accounted for 1.4 percent of total funding. Interestingly, Republican candidates raised only marginally more from PACs than Democratic candidates did: $1.6 million as against $1.5 million.

Candidates Dukakis, Hart, and du Pont refused to accept PAC contributions; Babbitt also refused, but somehow the FEC listed him as having received $1,000 from that source. Curiously, Robertson received only $8 to qualify for his listing. The FEC also calculated that presidential candidates received $2.3 million from other political committees (not PACs), primarily from joint fund-raising committees, from committees of candidates for Congress, and from miscellaneous sources.

TABLE 2.8
Political Action Committee Receipts: Presidential Prenomination Campaigns, 1988

Babbitt	$ 1,000
Biden	150
Dukakis	0
Gephardt	661,320
Gore	506,870
Hart	0
Jackson	46,400
LaRouche	5,000
Bush	670,567
Dole	848,931
du Pont	0
Haig	19,820
Kemp	64,998
Robertson	8
Total	$3,113,876

Source: Federal Election Commission.

An Overview

In the Democratic contests for nomination, the 7 candidates all needed exposure. Dukakis had the most money, enabling him to win by spending the most money; these funds gave him staying power through the long campaign season. Jesse Jackson had much more money than he had had in 1984 but received notable media attention throughout, with the consequence that spending was less important for him than for others; he won or came in second in several primaries or caucuses where he was outspent.

Pat Robertson showed in 1988 what George McGovern did in 1972—that a minority with strong feelings, if activated by an effective organization and supported by sufficient resources, can win or do well, particularly in caucus states, at less cost than is necessary in primary states.[26] Jackson also had an intensely loyal following but a less effective organization and fewer resources than Robertson.

One analysis of Super Tuesday indicates that the Democratic big spenders won in 62 percent of the states on that day, whereas the big spenders won in only 24 percent of the Republican contests.[27] As Clyde Wilcox has suggested, "Campaign spending matters most when little-known candidates contest the nomination, and matters considerably less when the candidates are well known and when free media provide voters with sufficient information to make up their minds."[28]

As noted in Chapter 6, only 6 percent of presidential prenomination spending was devoted to television. Not all candidates' television spending was divulged, and even less information was available on production costs. Table 2.9 summarizes the available data. Relatively low television spending in the primary and caucus period is explained by a number of factors. For example, retail politics in Iowa and New Hampshire stress personal campaigning and do not demand much

TABLE 2.9
Expenditures for Television Advertising: Selected 1988 Prenomination Campaigns

Candidate	Television Time	Production
Bush	$ 3,197,646	$ n/a
Dole	2,210,062	741,626
du Pont	1,200,000[a]	n/a
Kemp	2,290,900[a]	n/a
Dukakis	3,796,914	1,463,085
Total	$12,695,522	$2,204,711

[a]Breakdown between airing and production costs unavailable.

Source: Citizens' Research Foundation.

electronic advertising; in Iowa, TV costs are low, but in New Hampshire, such costs are too high because TV messages must be broadcast on Boston stations, making it difficult to stay within the state expenditure limit. On Super Tuesday, the remaining candidates' money was running low; political broadcasting occurred only in special circumstances, where focus was on a certain state or area, because overall there were too many media markets to cover in so many states.

The Mismanagement of Money: Gary Hart

On Saturday, March 12, 1988, Gary Hart withdrew from the Democratic contest for the second time. His first withdrawal had occurred in May of 1987, after the *Miami Herald* broke the story of his alleged relationship with a young model, Donna Rice. His second withdrawal came after he won just 1 percent of the Iowa caucus votes, 4 percent in the New Hampshire primary, and 3 percent of the Super Tuesday vote. By delaying the announcement of his second withdrawal until after the February 24 dispersal of federal matching funds, Hart's campaign collected more than $1 million from the presidential checkoff account.[29]

Before his first exit, Hart had raised nearly $2.2 million in the period from January to May 1987. His second withdrawal occurred in a radically different fund-raising environment: He raised only some $116,000 during December 1987 and January 1988.[30] Although Hart had been described as someone who "knows policy issues better than anyone else,"[31] he was plagued by money problems in both his campaigns for the presidency. These problems were not created solely by the scandal surrounding Donna Rice; they were part of a pattern of poor money management that had become evident in the Hart campaign style as early as his 1984 bid. The Hart campaign was an illustration of the importance of competent money management for any candidate.

The *New York Times* reported that "Mr. Hart's re-entry into the race was at times overshadowed by his continuing inability to pay off more than $1 million in debts from his 1984 bid. In addition, he had to respond to new allegations raised in newspaper accounts in January about irregularities in his 1984 campaign finances."[32] These irregularities centered around a Los Angeles videotape entrepreneur, Stuart Karl, Jr. According to one of Karl's employees, "Mr. Karl had been advised by Douglas Rosen, the [1984 Hart] campaign's finance director, to collect money from [his own] employees and reimburse them."[33] Karl was alleged to have funneled about $100,000 to Hart's campaign and to have written personal checks for thousands of dollars to cover routine campaign expenses. A media consultant to the 1984 campaign, Raymond

Strother, also raised funds. He later said, "It was like he [Hart] didn't want to know about the money. The truth is, Gary Hart had absolutely no idea about the money being raised in his campaign."[34]

After the U.S. attorney in Los Angeles asked the Federal Bureau of Investigation to look into the matter, the Hart campaign admitted it had received such illegal contributions in 1984 and would attempt to refund the money to Stuart Karl's employees. However, Hart's 1988 campaign manager, Susan Casey, admitted that "since the 1984 campaign is $1.1 million in debt, all that could be done was to add the questionable contributors to the list of debtors to be repaid."[35]

On March 25, 1988, the FEC ruled that Hart could not use any leftover 1988 campaign funds to repay his 1984 debts until the 1988 books had been audited and all questions about their propriety resolved, a process that could take many months.[36] Hart's 1984 debt was originally pegged at $4.8 million, but some creditors, including Stuart Karl, had been persuaded to take as little as ten cents on the dollar. By the 1988 campaign, the 1984 debt had shrunk to a little more than $1.1 million. Hart's 1984 creditors proved a continual embarrassment during the 1988 bid; in one instance, federal marshals were called in by one creditor to seize money at a fund-raiser for California big givers.[37] Two other creditors tried without success to seize a $100,000 certificate of deposit.[38] Thus, two problems related to money management—the 1984 debt and the surfacing of the Stuart Karl story—combined to help push Hart out of the 1988 race for the last time.

Stuart Karl pleaded guilty to conspiring to violate federal election laws in a felony plea bargain. He was fined $60,000 for making excessive contributions to Gary Hart's 1984 campaign and to several Democratic Senate campaigns, and he was placed on probation for three years for conspiring to defraud the government in making $185,000 in political contributions, far beyond the $1,000 limit. He also agreed to cooperate in further investigations.[39]

FINANCING THE NATIONAL CONVENTIONS

The second phase of the presidential selection process, the national nominating conventions, was financed by public funds provided to the two major parties—$9.2 million each. But the Atlanta convention cost more than twice as much—$22.5 million—with the remainder provided by the city and host committees. Atlanta assembled a financial package to attract the convention to the city, and the city government dedicated a special tax levied on hotel guests for the purpose. This enabled the host committee, the Atlanta '88 Committee, to borrow $5 million from two Atlanta banks, which became the largest creditors. The loans are being paid off by revenues from the tax. Table 2.10 presents expenditures that account for a substantial portion of the overall costs covered by the 1988 Democratic National Convention Committee, Inc. and the host committee. Examples of convention expenditures only partially covered in Table 2.10 included $3.5 million in construction costs and more than $3 million in state, county, and city security costs.[40]

The Republican convention in New Orleans cost at least $18 million, covered by $9.2 million in federal subsidy, coupled with support from the City of New Orleans and host committees, mainly corporate in source. An accounting of the spending of the $9.2 million federal grant is shown in Table 2.11.

Host committee funds for both the Atlanta and New Orleans conventions were raised privately, in amounts as large as $100,000, primarily from corporate sponsors. Ironically, the public funding was designed to provide an alternative to private funds, but the latter still can be raised under increasingly easy guidelines. Every four years since public funding went into effect in 1976, the Federal Election Commission has interpreted the law to permit more and more private money for operating the conventions and has exempted more and more expenditures from the spending limits.

TABLE 2.10
Democratic National Convention, 1988 (Atlanta, Georgia)

Expenditure	Amount
Administration	$ 4,596,857
Transportation	988,022
Office and media space	1,798,586
Hotels	213,711
Food	131,283
Telecommunications	411,489
Platform, rules, and other commissions	1,068,280
Convention secretary	306,841
Medical and fire services	-0-
Media, communications, and public relations	541,904
Seating	87,215
Construction	1,620,962
VIPs	103,555
Security	857,342
Credentials	272,085
TV production	1,843,584
Computer services	348,330
Host committee	998,227
Program book, research, and special projects	504,376
Total	$15,731,197

Source: Citizens' Research Foundation.

TABLE 2.11
Republican National Convention, 1988 (New Orleans, Louisiana)

Site selection costs	$ 171,201
Rules committee	13,317
Platform committee	232,411
Arrangements committee	216,376
Special organizations	285,551
Administration	1,397,034
Convention services	580,214
Media—logistics	155,323
Superdome—operations	1,331,394
Superdome—programs	1,559,847
Convention management	3,237,805
Total	$9,180,473

Source: Citizens' Research Foundation.

State and local governments where the conventions are held are permitted to provide certain services and facilities, such as convention halls, transportation, and security, the costs of which are not counted against the parties' expenditure limits. Parties may accept such items as free hotel rooms and conference facilities as long as other groups holding conventions of comparable size and duration are offered similar benefits. (No other conventions really approximate the mega-size of the political conventions.) Local businesses and national corporations with local outlets may contribute funds to host committees or civic associations seeking to attract or assist the political conventions, as long as they can reasonably expect a commensurate commercial return during the life of the convention.[41]

The Republican party held its 1984 convention in Dallas. State law and long-standing local tradition prevented the use of tax revenue and other government moneys to finance convention-related costs. Accordingly, the city sought and received an FEC ruling that it could establish and administer a nonprofit, nonpartisan convention fund to finance facilities and services for the convention, provided the fund pay for such items and services at their fair market value. The ruling stated that payments made to the city-administered fund for convention facilities and services and donations made to the fund would not constitute contributions to the Republican National Committee and would not count against the committee's convention spending ceiling.[42]

Consequently, the convention fund was able to collect donations in unlimited amounts from individuals, associations, businesses, and corporations and did not have to disclose the names of contributors. The Internal Revenue Service also ruled that contributions to the Dallas convention fund would be fully tax deductible.[43] In 1983, San Francisco, site of the 1984 Democratic National Convention, received a similar FEC ruling for its Convention Promotion Services Fund.[44]

Similarly, the 1988 conventions were financed in part by corporate and other large contributions, combined with the grants of federal public funds and supplemented by Atlanta and New Orleans public funds. The FEC gave General Motors and other automobile manufacturers permission to lend, through local dealerships, fleets of autos for transporting important and elected officials at the conventions—estimated to have cost General Motors at least $350,000.[45] Both parties also were able to arrange reduced-cost services by agreeing to designate airlines and others as "official suppliers" for the conventions. Costly lounges to which delegates were invited to relax with their corporate, labor, and trade association hosts were evident at both conventions.

Among the $100,000 corporate and labor contributors to the Democratic convention were Great Western Resources, The Henley Group, American Federation of State, County and Municipal Employees, Machinists Non-Partisan Political League, and the National Education Association.[46] Among the $100,000 corporate contributors to the Republican convention were American Express, American Petrofina, ARCO, Brown-Forman, Chevron, Coca-Cola, Delta Airlines, Dresser Industries, PepsiCo, RJR Nabisco, and Southern Company.[47]

The mix of public and private financing (including tax-exempt funding) for the nominating conventions satisfies the parties because it provides sufficient moneys and involves local participation. But the development every four years of new means of introducing private money clouds the premise in the 1974 law that public funding would essentially replace private funds. Each year, the FEC has opened more avenues for private—often corporate and labor—funds. Besides questioning the rationale for the use of public funds, the infusion of large amounts of private dollars makes the accompanying expenditure limits meaningless.

RECOMMENDATIONS FOR FUTURE CONVENTION FUNDING

After the 1988 conventions, a bipartisan Commission on National Political Conventions was formed to study the adequacy of the present convention system. The commission was cochaired by Frank Fahrenkopf, Jr., former chairman of the Republican National Committee, and former Democratic National Committee chairman Charles T. Manatt. Their report, issued June 7, 1990, contained—among other proposals, mainly related to televised proceedings—the following recommendations concerning the funding of national conventions:

1. The Commission strongly recommends continued use of the check-off method for the funding of conventions. The Commission also recommends a cooperative public relations effort by the Democratic and Republican parties to encourage greater use of the presidential campaign funding check-off on the federal tax return by the voting public.
2. The Commission recommends that the Federal Election Commission examine closely the amount of funds designated for the use of the parties for their 1992 conventions, considering the expected rise in costs due to inflation and the ongoing burden of additional costs placed upon the host cities. The Commission recommends funds for the political conventions be increased appropriately.[48]

NOTES

1. Public Law 92–225, 86 Stat. 3 (1973) (codified as amended in 2 U.S.C. 431 et seq., and in scattered sections of 18 and 47 U.S.C.).
2. Public Law 92–178, Sections 701–703, 801–802, 85 Stat. 497, 560–574 (1972) (codified as amended in scattered sections of 26 U.S.C.).
3. Public Law 93–443, 88 Stat. 1263 (codified in scattered sections of U.S.C.).
4. Public Law 94–283, 90 Stat. 475 (codified in scattered sections of U.S.C.).
5. Public Law 96–187.
6. *Buckley* v. *Valeo,* 424 U.S. 1 (1976).
7. For a thorough analysis of the impact of federal campaign finance laws on the conduct of the 1984 presidential campaigns, see Herbert E. Alexander and Brian A. Haggerty, *Financing the 1984 Election* (Lexington, Mass.: Lexington Books, 1987).
8. Ibid., pp. 84–88.
9. "Presidential Pre-nomination Campaigns," *FEC Report on Financial Activity, 1987–1988,* Final Report, Federal Election Commission, August 1989, tables A6, A7, pp. 9–10, and appendix 1, unnumbered. The figures used in this text include 1989 expenditures through June 30, 1989.
10. "President Bush's Campaign Finance Proposals," the White House, press release, June 29, 1989, pp. 1–4.
11. Anthony Corrado, "The Pre-Candidacy PAC Loophole," *Boston Globe,* May 6, 1990.
12. Ibid.
13. Ibid.
14. Ibid.
15. "FEC May Review Rules Governing Foreign Ownership of Corporations Sponsoring PACs," *Campaign Practices Reports,* June 25, 1990, p. 4.
16. Democrats alleged that Bush not only exceeded the spending limit but also offset certain expenditures in the weeks before the Republican convention by designating them as Republican "party-building" expenses or as official government expenses incurred in his capacity as vice president. See "Democrats Claim Bush Exceeds Campaign Spending Limit," *PACs & Lobbies,* August 17,

1989, p. 11. Much of the textual formulation is based on Herbert E. Alexander, "The Price We Pay for Our Presidents," *Public Opinion,* vol. 11, no. 6, March/April 1989, pp. 46–48.

17. "FEC Announces Spending Limits for 1988 Presidential Race," Federal Election Commission, press release, February 5, 1988, pp. 1–2.

18. Richard L. Berke, "Election Unit Eases TV Ad Limit, Rejecting Advice of Own Counsel," *New York Times,* February 26, 1988.

19. L. Sandy Maisel, "Spending Patterns in Presidential Nominating Campaigns, 1976–1988," paper prepared for the American Political Science Association Annual Meeting, Washington, D.C., September 1–4, 1988, p. 21.

20. "FEC Approves Matching Funds for 1988 Presidential Candidates," Federal Election Commission, press release, March 8, 1989.

21. Clyde Wilcox, "Financing the 1988 Prenomination Campaigns," manuscript, p. 18 (available at the Citizens' Research Foundation, Los Angeles, Calif.).

22. Ibid., p. 20.

23. Brian Sullam, "The Cash Campaign," *New Republic,* March 14, 1988, pp. 9–13.

24. *Campaign Reporter,* vol. 2, no. 1, January 1990, p. 5.

25. "Presidential Prenomination Campaigns," op. cit., table A1, p. 2.

26. Maisel, op. cit., p. 21.

27. Michael Robinson, Clyde Wilcox, and Paul Marshall, "The Presidency: Not for Sale," *Public Opinion,* vol. 11, no. 6, March/April 1989, p. 52.

28. Wilcox, op. cit., p. 2.

29. Maureen Dowd, "Hart, Conceding People Decided, Quits Again," *New York Times,* March 12, 1988.

30. Tamara Jones, "Hart Ends Race, Saying He 'Got a Fair Hearing'," *Los Angeles Times,* March 12, 1988.

31. Ibid.

32. Dowd, op. cit.

33. Richard L. Berke, "Campaign Finances of '84 Haunt Hart in '88," *New York Times,* January 30, 1988.

34. Ibid.

35. Ibid.

36. David Lauter, "Panel Limits Hart in Using '88 Funds to Pay '84 Debts," *Los Angeles Times,* March 25, 1988.

37. Ibid.

38. "2 Hart Creditors Lose a Decision on His '84 Debt," *New York Times,* January 2, 1988.

39. Annette Haddad, "Video Promotor Fired for Illegal Campaign Contributions," United Press International teletype, December 7, 1988.

40. Scott Shephard, "Cost of the Democratic Convention Will Reach At Least $22.4 Million," *Atlanta Constitution,* September 30, 1988.

41. Alexander and Haggerty, op. cit., p. 291.

42. Ibid., pp. 291–292.

43. Ibid., pp. 297–298.

44. Ibid., pp. 302–305.

45. "General Motors' Generosity: 250 Cars Per Convention," *PACs & Lobbies,* July 20, 1988, pp. 1, 4; also Brooks Jackson, "Big Business Is Back in Thick of Things at the Conventions," *Wall Street Journal,* August 16, 1988.

46. Derived from listings of $100,000 contributions made in June 1988 or earlier, in "Report of Non-Federal Receipts and Disbursements," *Democratic News,* August 15, 1988.

47. Brooks Jackson, op. cit.; and Richard L. Berke, "Companies Supply Parties' Lifeblood," *New York Times,* August 16, 1988.

48. "Reaching the American Voter: Party Conventions and the Television Electorate," *Final Report of the Commission on National Political Conventions,* The Center for Democracy, Washington, D.C., 1990, p. 8.

3

FINANCING THE PRESIDENTIAL ELECTIONS: THE GENERAL ELECTION CAMPAIGNS

The Democratic nomination went to Dukakis in mid-July, giving him an extra month before Bush's nomination in mid-August. Dukakis therefore had to spread out the use of his money over a longer time until the November election, but Bush was able to concentrate his general election spending over a shorter period. Bush's major media spending did not begin until mid-September, after he took the lead in the public opinion polls from Dukakis's preconvention status.

Spending on broadcast media in the prenomination campaigns accounted for about 6 percent of the $212 million total expenditure. But in the general election, the Bush campaign spent more than $30 million on media, and the Dukakis campaign spent less than $30 million; however, both spent nearly 50 percent of the public grants they received. In a sense, general election public funding amounts to a major transfer of funds from the government to the broadcasters. Of course, the broadcasters provided significant additional free time in the form of presidential debates, daily coverage, and special programs.

BUSH-QUAYLE MEDIA SPENDING

The Bush-Quayle media expenditures, totaling $31.5 million apart from additional production costs, are shown in Table 3.1. They represent a large increase over the $22.9 million spent by the Reagan-Bush ticket four years earlier. The network costs were less than half of the spot announcement costs; like the five-minute programs, the spots were broadcast in key markets only. The network costs included election eve broadcasts on three networks.[1]

DUKAKIS-BENTSEN MEDIA SPENDING

The Dukakis-Bentsen media expenditures, totaling $23,550,000 not counting additional production costs, are shown in Table 3.2. The

TABLE 3.1
Bush-Quayle Media Expenditures, General Election, 1988

	Amounts
Television	
Network	$ 9,212,500
Spot announcements	19,377,500
Cable	1,331,800
5-Minute	306,800
Subtotal	$30,228,600
Radio	1,229,700
Grand Total	$31,458,300

Source: Citizens' Research Foundation.

TABLE 3.2
Dukakis-Bentsen Media Expenditures, General Election, 1988

Television	
Network	
Regional network	
Cable	$ 7,000,000
5-minute spots	
Spot	14,600,000
Unwired news net	650,000
Total television	$22,250,000
Radio	1,100,000
Print	200,000
Total net media	$23,550,000

Source: Citizens' Research Foundation.

categories are not identical to the Bush-Quayle breakdown, and the total is considerably less than the $31.5 million figure for the winning campaign. The spot announcement costs were more than twice as much as the combined costs for networks, cable, and five-minute programs. Radio expenditures were in a cost range similar to that of the Bush-Quayle campaign.

SOFT MONEY

In the general election phase of the presidential selection process, the most notable financial phenomenon was the search for soft money. Soft money is raised and spent outside the restraints of federal law and is determined by state laws, many of which are less stringent than federal law. Efforts by the campaigns to raise soft money became as competitive and as high profile as the search for votes on November 8.

Soft money was sanctioned by the 1979 amendments to the Federal Election Campaign Act. It was raised and spent in the 1980 and 1984 presidential campaigns, but the money was raised in low-key efforts (not in the high-visibility, competitive ways of 1988) and in smaller amounts,[2] as shown in Table 3.3.

Both parties at the national level sought, through parallel fund-raising efforts carried on by the candidates' prenomination campaign operatives, soft money contributions to supplement the public funds each presidential and vice presidential ticket received: $46.1 million, plus $8.3 million that the national parties could spend on behalf of the ticket, to be supplemented by however much hard and soft money the parties raised and spent. Money was raised centrally at a frantic pace as if no public funding or expenditure limits existed. It was raised not by the parties but by the same Bush and Dukakis finance people who solicited the candidates' prenomination funds. And it was raised in large individual contributions—much in excess of the federal contribution limitations—some as much as $100,000 each; the Republicans claimed 267 contributors of $100,000 or more, and the Democrats counted 130 individuals who gave or raised $100,000.[3]

TABLE 3.3
Soft Money Expenditures, 1980–1988 (in millions)

Year	Republican	Democrat
1980	$15.1	$ 4.0
1984	15.6	6.0
1988	22.0	23.0

Source: Citizens' Research Foundation.

Robert A. Farmer, treasurer of the Dukakis-Bentsen campaign, started the drive for soft money by announcing an effort to raise $50 million in such private donations. He later admitted this was a strategic error because it triggered a Republican response in the form of Team 100, which raised $22 million in soft money.[4]

Michael Dukakis put a $100,000 limit on soft money amounts that would be accepted and refused to take any from corporations, labor unions, or PACs. However, before he was nominated, the Democrats had accepted soft money from corporate and labor sources for help in funding the Democratic National Convention (DNC). Most Republican soft money contributions were from individuals—one of those disclosed was as high as $503,263, contributed by the former ambassador to Hungary, Nicholas Salgo—but some were corporate.[5] Some Republican soft money was raised in amounts as low as $1,000 for tickets to the "Gala Luncheon" at the Republican National Convention. The costs of the gala were part of the Republican soft money expenditures. So, both conventions used up some of the soft money expenditures for 1988 shown in Table 3.3, which also compares 1988 with 1984 and 1980. Additional hard money (within the restraints of federal law) in the tens of millions was raised and spent by both Republicans and Democrats on combined hard-soft money activities related to the presidential campaigns. And additional soft money was raised and spent locally by state and local party committees in amounts not included in the national soft money totals; a detailed study of soft money at the national and state levels is reported in Chapter 5.

The Dukakis Campaign

The Dukakis campaign claims to have raised $52 million from June 1 on, categorized as:

Direct mail	$18.3 million
Events	18.3 million
Trustees	15.4 million

These figures include the joint Dukakis-Democratic National Committee fund-raising and listed 350,000 contributors, with an average of $160 per contribution. They combine both hard and soft money.

The extent of elite fund-raising in the Dukakis campaign is underlined by numbers of active solicitors:

- 1,284 finance committee members committed to give or raise $10,000
- 248 board of directors members committed to give or raise $25,000

- 292 trustees committed to give or raise $100,000.

Although there may be some overlap or unfulfilled quotas, the numbers are impressive, and they are the reason that Dukakis ran the best-financed campaign the Democrats have put on in many years. The regional and top state totals follow:

Regional totals (non-direct mail)

New England	$ 6,282,428
Mid-Atlantic	11,399,700
South	4,935,947
Midwest	3,536,237
West	7,203,903

Top 10 states (non-direct mail)

California	$ 6,128,581
New York	6,021,121
Massachusetts	5,014,093
Washington, D.C.	2,189,058
Texas	1,759,461
Illinois	1,713,708
New Jersey	1,108,626
Ohio	1,042,918
Florida	933,000
Michigan	756,782

Dukakis direct mail fund-raising, combined with that of the Democratic National Committee after June 1, showed a total income of more than $18 million, an average gift of $46, and a response rate of 4.8 percent. Total fund-raising costs were $8.1 million.

Thus, the 1988 general election period, in which candidate spending limits were set by law at $46.1 million, found more than twice as much spent, mainly by combinations of candidate and party committees at the state and local levels. The erosion of the effectiveness of the contribution and expenditure limits represents a return to big money—public and private, hard and soft, candidate and party. It threatens the general election public funding concept—that full public funding would be provided, with minimal national party participation and effective expenditure limitations. Public funds were intended to help provide or supply in entirety the money serious candidates need to present themselves and their ideas to the electorate. Such public money also was meant to diminish or eliminate the need for financing from wealthy donors and interest groups, thereby minimizing the influence contributors possibly could exert on officeholders. And, of course, public funding was designed to relieve candidates of the need to engage in fund-raising. But instead, they helped to raise soft money. If soft money expenditures do violence to the rationale for public funding, the whole election law framework is opened to doubt.

Moreover, when presidential candidates accept public financing for the general election campaign, they agree not to raise private funds nor to spend more money than permitted under the expenditure limits. Yet, the presidential candidates speak at events at which soft money is raised, and their finance staffs from the prenomination campaigns help to raise soft money and direct its disbursements in key states. Some observers believe this is a violation of the law.

There is much criticism of soft money, but it plays an important role in both voter outreach and party renewal.[6] Required by federal law to be restricted to spending related to voluntary activities, its purpose is to allow state and local party committees to undertake such activities as registration and get-out-the-vote drives, phone banks, and the like— widely accepted functions that attract the citizen participation that is highly valued in a democracy. Soft money also can be used for items such as bumper strips and local canvassing materials. With more money available in 1988, the definition of voluntary activity was broadened by experience to include joint state headquarters and related expenses shared with presidential campaign operatives in key states. (See the California experience discussed in Chapter 5.) In contrast, the public funding provided by tax checkoffs to the candidates was used directly on advertising by the presidential tickets. To some extent, soft money expenditures freed up more of the public money for advertising, travel, and other expenditures directly associated with the presidential campaigns.

THREE PARALLEL CAMPAIGNS

In the 1988 general election, the campaigns both expressed a need for a level playing field. As a result, both sought to supplement spending beyond the expenditure limits through the use of soft money. But soft money was only one component of spending outside such limits. Analysis of the presidential general election period demonstrates that at least three distinct but parallel campaigns were conducted, either by each candidate or on each candidate's behalf. Amounts of each component are shown in Table 3.4.

In the first campaign, spending was limited by law to the flat-grant amounts—$46.1 million that public funding provided. This money was supplemented by national-party-coordinated expenditures of $8.3 million. The total of these public and party funds—$54.4 million—was entirely within the control of the major party nominees and their campaign organizations. And identical amounts were spent by the Bush-

TABLE 3.4
Sources of Funds, Major Party Presidential Candidates, 1988 General Election
(in millions)

	Sources of Funds	Bush	Dukakis
Limited campaign			
	Federal grant	$46.1	$ 46.1
Candidate controlled	National party	8.3	8.3
Unlimited campaign			
	State and local party	22.0[a]	23.0
	Labor[b]	5.0	25.0
Candidate may coordinate	Corporate/association[b]	1.5	1.0
	Compliance	4.0	2.5
Independent of candidate	Independent expenditures[c]	6.8	.6
Total		$93.7	$106.5

[a] Includes money raised by the national party committee and channeled to state and local party committees.
[b] Includes internal communication costs (both those in excess of $2,000, which are reported as required by law, and those of $2,000 or less, which are not required to be reported, registration and voter turnout expenditures, overhead, and other related costs.
[c] Does not include amounts spent to oppose the candidates: $2.7 million against Dukakis, $77,325 against Bush, and $63,103 against Quayle.

Source: Citizens' Research Foundation.

Quayle and Dukakis-Bentsen campaigns in these categories. The ways in which the Republicans spent their coordinated expenditures follow:

Media costs	$6,954,961
Polling	158,726
Election night expenses	12,000
Printing/mailing costs	294,558
Telemarketing	854,589
Surrogate speaker program	14,348
Total	$8,289,182

The media costs are part of the $31.5 million Bush-Quayle total reported earlier.

In the second campaign, spending was provided for but not limited under the law. Some of it was directly controlled by the nominees and their campaign organizations, and some was outside their control. Even those funds outside their direct control, however, could be coordinated with spending by the nominees. This second campaign was financed in part by funds raised under FECA limits from private contributors to pay the legal, accounting, and related costs the organization incurred in complying with the law. It also was financed by soft money funds spent by state and local party committees—in almost identical amounts by each major party. In addition, funds were spent on behalf of the nominees by labor unions, trade associations, and membership groups, used for partisan communications with their own constituencies and on nominally nonpartisan activities directed to the general public. For example, it was reported that Senator Alan Cranston (D–CA) raised $12 million for tax-exempt groups carrying out voter registration and turnout drives among Democatic-leaning groups[7]—some of this activity later became a matter of controversy in the savings and loan scandal, as reported in Chapter 5. This parallel spending could be coordinated with spending by the nominees' campaign organizations.

In the third campaign, spending also was provided for but not limited under the law. Under *Buckley* v. *Valeo,* individuals and groups are permitted to spend unlimited amounts to advocate the election or defeat of specific candidates as long as these independent expenditures are made without consultation or collaboration with the candidates or their campaigns. The advantage to the Bush campaign in independent expenditures was notable and contrasted with the $2.8 million spent in opposition to Dukakis, as shown in detail in Chapter 5.

These three parallel campaigns illustrate why expenditure limits are illusory in a pluralistic system with numerous openings for disbursement sanctioned by law or court decisions. Such developments demonstrate the difficulties in attempting to regulate money strictly in the American political arena. When freedom of speech and association are guaranteed, restricting money at any given point in the campaign process results in new channels being carved through which monied individuals and groups can seek to bring their influence to bear on campaigns and officeholders.

With totals of $93.7 million for or on behalf of Bush and $106.5 million for or on behalf of Dukakis, as shown in Table 3.4, it is apparent that the candidates' spending limitations, plus those of the national party, are not effective. Moreover, the perceived need for additional spending by both campaigns was apparent. The total amounts spent in the major party general election campaigns were remarkable, not only in terms of the aggregate amounts raised and spent on behalf of the candidates but also because the Democratic candidate was the beneficiary of more spending than was the Republican. This stark reversal from all presidential elections in the twentieth century occurred for several reasons: (1) Unlike the situation in 1980 or 1984, in 1988 the Democrats spent the full amount of party-coordinated expenditures,

$8.3 million; (2) in 1988, the Democrats spent slightly more than the Republicans in soft money, reversing the experience in 1980 and 1984; and (3) the Democrats continued their advantage of strong labor spending in parallel campaigns, amounting to $25 million. Indeed, the Democrats achieved more than their long-sought-after level playing field; they actually had a slight advantage in dollars spent.

REEVALUATING REFORM

If the system of public funding for presidential campaigns is to survive, it is necessary to consider making changes in order to keep up with actual campaign costs in terms of contribution and expenditure limits and the amounts of public funding.

Although the federally imposed individual contribution limit of $1,000 per candidate per election may seem high to many Americans who could not make such a gift, the erosion of the dollar has been so severe that a $1,000 contribution in 1988 was worth about $400 in 1975 value, when the limit went into effect; in other words, when adjusted to reflect increases in the Consumer Price Index, it cost $2,246 in 1988 dollars to buy what $1,000 would purchase in 1975.[8]

Yet, the costs of most items needed in campaigns skyrocketed at a much higher rate. For example, from 1984 to 1988, the cost of a thirty-second commercial during a top-rated television show in Des Moines rose about 64 percent, to some $1,800 from approximately $1,000.[9] Costs of thirty-second spots in larger media markets were as high as $25,000 in Los Angeles, for example, during World Series broadcasts, as shown in Chapter 6.

The feasibility of public financing has depended on the taxpayers' willingness to earmark a small portion of their tax liabilities—$1 for individuals and $2 for married persons filing jointly—for the Presidential Election Campaign Fund by using the federal income tax checkoff. But the $1 checkoff level has not been increased since its inception in 1972. Until now, the system has provided more than enough money to cover the public funds certified to presidential prenomination and general election candidates and to the major parties for their national nominating conventions: Certifications by the Federal Election Commission totaled $70.9 million in 1976, $100.6 million in 1980, $133.1 million in 1984, and $177.8 million in 1988. The 1988 public financing payouts in the three phases of the presidential selection process were shown earlier in Table 2.6.

However, the high rate of growth in spending has resulted in a level of government payouts that exceeds the amount of revenue generated by the system. Table 3.5 shows that, from 1973 through 1989, the

TABLE 3.5
Federal Income Tax Checkoff

Calendar Year	Percentage of Returns with Checkoff[a]	Amounts Checked Off
1989	20.1	$32,285,646
1988	21.0	33,013,987
1987	21.7	33,651,947
1986	23.0	35,753,837
1985	23.0	35,036,761
1984	23.7	34,712,761
1983	24.2	35,631,068
1982	27.0	39,023,882
1981	28.7	41,049,052
1980	27.4	38,838,417
1979	25.4	35,941,347
1978	28.6	39,246,689
1977	27.5	36,606,008
1976	25.5	33,731,945
1975	24.2	31,656,525
1974	—[b]	27,591,546
1973	7.0	2,427,000

[a] The percentages refer to returns of the previous year, e.g., the 27 percent of 1981 tax returns that indicated a one- or two-dollar checkoff directed $39,023,882 into the Presidential Election Campaign Fund in calendar year 1982.
[b] The 1973 returns were the first to have the campaign fund checkoff on the first page. To compensate for the presumed difficulty of locating the separate form in the previous year, taxpayers were permitted to check off $1 for 1972 as well as 1973. Because this option did not exist in any other year, percentage figures for those returns would be misleading.

Source: Federal Election Commission.

approximate percentage of tax returns checking off money for the Presidential Election Campaign Fund has ranged from a high of 28.7 percent in 1980 to a low of 20.1 percent in 1988. Based on estimates of future spending and revenue collection, the FEC projects that the 1992 campaign will have to use more than half of the surplus funds available in order to meet its costs and that by 1996 the system will be unable to meet costs, resulting in a $71 million deficit.[10]

The experience in 1988 raises serious questions about the adequacy of the amounts of public funding the candidates received to enable them to compete effectively in both the pre- and postnomination campaigns. And the public funding for the conventions is clearly inadequate. Increases in the rate of the tax checkoff, in the amounts of the public funding allocations, and in the overall expenditure limits are not only necessary but justified. New ways of defining and dealing with soft money and seeing that, at the least, it is fully disclosed are needed. New consideration of the appropriate role of political party committees, which spend most of the soft money, surely is called for. And independent expenditure campaigns can perhaps be better regulated.

It is possible that the high spending in 1988 will trigger a search for further reform. Or the 1988 experience could add ammunition to the effort of some U.S. senators to repeal both public funding and expenditure limits, on grounds that the system has reverted to prereform days of large contributors and escalating costs. If such large amounts of money are raised in the private sector, they ask, why provide public dollars?

When moneys spent on both of the conventions and the general election are twice as much as envisioned by spending limits, the time is at hand to reappraise the effectiveness of the law. The public funding, however, could be conceptualized as "floors without ceilings," that is, as giving financial assistance that will permit candidates to have access to the electorate but not exact the accompanying price of spending limits. But this is not a popular view. The notion of "floors without ceilings" has its supporters among some academics and others, but it has not gained popular acceptance; of course, most foreign nations that provide public funds do so without imposing expenditure limits. However, members of Congress will ask why we should add tax dollars to unlimited private dollars. In the circumstances, then, most will interpret the spending as excessive and as indicating a breakdown of the system envisioned by the Congress when it enacted public funding in the 1971 Federal Election Campaign Act and the 1974 amendments. But "floors without ceilings" well describes what was actually experienced in 1988. The development of a campaign cost index, on which a revised system of public funding and expenditure limits could be pegged, would be an important first step.

Yet, despite the high spending and the negative campaigns, any evaluation of the system should conclude that voluntarily donated campaign funds and public funds earmarked by taxpayers to help finance campaigns should be considered money well spent. The most costly campaigns are those in which voters choose poorly because they are ill-informed. For a candidate or party, however, the most expensive election is a lost election. Accordingly, candidates and parties often spend as much as they can—and sometimes go into debt.

CONCLUSIONS

The FECA has achieved mixed results, if the experience of four presidential campaigns is any indication. In the prenomination period, the public funding provisions have improved access to the contest by supplementing the treasuries of candidates without the backing of wealthy contributors. Evidence may be found in the victorious campaign of initially little-known Jimmy Carter in 1976, in the ability of George Bush and John Anderson to wage effective campaigns in 1980, and in the fact that Gary Hart and Jesse Jackson made their marks in 1984, as Jackson again did in 1988. And in the 1988 prenomination period, several little-known Democrats needed the public money to gain essential prominence.

Prior to 1988, the law's contribution limits were thought to have reduced the possibility that wealthy contributors could exert political influence. Its disclosure provisions resulted in more campaign finance information being available to the public than ever before, and its compliance requirements caused campaigns to place greater emphasis on money management and accountability. These effects suggest that, in some ways, the laws succeeded in altering the behavior of candidates, committees, and contributors to achieve some of the goals of campaign reform. But the incidence and amounts of soft money in 1988 had implications for the effectiveness of both contribution and spending limits.

Still another result of the law has been less favorable. The low individual contribution limit has replaced wealthy contributors with a variety of fund-raisers upon whom candidates may become equally dependent for campaign funds. The large contributor, in effect, has been replaced by the large solicitor. Solicitors include direct mail consultants with access to mailing lists of proven campaign donors; PAC managers with their increasingly sophisticated means of fund-raising; entertainment industry promoters who can persuade their clients to hold benefit concerts for favored candidates; and elite solicitors who can tap into networks of individuals capable of contributing up to the maximum allowed.

Even with public matching funds, the low contribution limit makes it difficult for candidates to raise sufficient money to conduct their campaigns. In 1984, for example, every eligible Democratic candidate ended his prenomination campaign with a substantial debt, and the combined indebtedness for all those candidates reached as high as $15 million. Debt repayment activities continued throughout the general election period—and well beyond—distracting attention and draining resources from the Democratic campaign. Although few 1988 campaigns had lingering debts, the low contribution limits required candidates to spend considerable time raising money. As of June 30, 1989, only $1,913,861 in debts was owed by the 1988 campaigns.

The low individual contribution limit and the expenditure limits have reduced campaign flexibility and rigidified the campaign process.

The contribution limit tends to work to the advantage of well-known candidates capable of raising money quickly, such as Bush, forcing lesser-known candidates to begin their fund-raising early, thereby lengthening the campaign season. The expenditure limit makes it difficult for candidates who have spent close to the maximum allowed to alter campaign strategy to fend off new challenges or take other new developments, such as Super Tuesday, into account. The spending limit also tends to encourage candidates to favor mass media advertising, which may be more cost effective than grass-roots campaigning but may not be as informative. It has caused candidates to centralize control of their campaigns at the expense of local authority. And cash flow and cash management problems abound.

The limits also have spurred the creation of several alternative means of avoidance, including presidential PACs, delegate committees, soft money, and independent expenditures. Restricting money at any given point in the campaign process often results in the development of new channels through which monied individuals and groups can seek to bring their influence to bear once more.

Despite the increase in campaign finance information available to the public because of the FECA's disclosure provisions, there has been some significant erosion in the ability of these provisions to bring important data to light. For example, in December 1983, the FEC voted 4 to 2 to allow candidates who contract with outside consultants on conducting campaign-related activities on their behalf to meet their disclosure obligations merely by reporting any payments made to those consultants.[11] The decision allowed the Mondale for President Committee to avoid public disclosure of its itemized media costs; instead, the committee merely had to report the lump sums it paid to its media firm. The commission failed to heed a warning from its own legal staff that, under such a ruling, campaigns could defeat the purpose of public disclosure of all campaign expenditures simply by contracting with a professional consulting firm to conduct campaign activities on their behalf and then reporting only the sums paid directly to that firm.

The Robertson campaign in 1987–1988 took advantage of the ruling by making a few large payments, including more than $3 million to one Arizona firm—Victory Communications International—for implementing a program to collect three million signatures on a petition urging Robertson to become a candidate; the campaign fund reports itemized only the expenditures to the company, without detailing how the money was spent. The campaign also refused to divulge details of the spending. Late in 1988, it was fined $25,000 by the FEC for failing to file in a timely fashion reports on these and related activities, which the FEC found constituted a candidacy more than a year before Robertson actually announced.[12]

Finally, the complexities of the law's compliance requirements have contributed to the professionalization of campaigns, possibly chilling enthusiasm for volunteer citizen participation in politics.

In the general election, public funding, combined with a ban on private contributions to the major party nominees—except to defray compliance costs—was intended to equalize spending between major party candidates, to control or limit campaign spending, and to eliminate the possibility of large individual or interest group contributions influencing presidential election results. In 1976, with a few exceptions, those goals appeared to have been achieved. But in 1980 and again in 1984 and 1988, due in large part to increased familiarity with the law's provisions as well as some changes in the law, political partisans discovered a variety of ways to upset the balance and reintroduce substantial amounts of private money into the campaigns: soft money contributions to state and local party committees to pay for activities beneficial to the presidential candidates; contributions to tax-exempt organizations conducting nominally nonpartisan voter drives that actually were intended to benefit a given party's candidate; independent expenditures; and spending by labor unions and other activities in parallel campaigns designed to help candidates.

Thus, putting together all the sources of spending shown in Table 3.4 demonstrates that the general election costs of $93.7 million for or on behalf of Bush and $106.5 million for or on behalf of Dukakis are well above the $54.4 million the law permitted the candidates and national committees to spend.

A statement of recommendations prepared by a number of 1988 presidential finance officers is offered in the appendix as an alternative set of ideas on this topic.

NOTES

1. *Campaign Reporter,* vol. 2, no. 1, January 1990, p. 6.

2. Herbert E. Alexander, "Soft Money," *Vox Pop Newsletter of Political Organizations and Parties,* vol. 8, no. 1, 1989, pp. 1–3, 7.

3. Paul Houston, "Bush, Dukakis Got Record Big Gifts," *Los Angeles Times,* December 10, 1988. The numbers need explanation: Not every contributor credited with a $100,000 contribution gave it all in soft money. Some had contributed up to $20,000, the legal limit, in hard money to the parties' national committees. Some gave directly to state central committees or in some other combination of hard and soft money totaling $100,000 and therefore were credited with that amount. Those contributors who were listed were really

$100,000 donors, but their donations were not necessarily all in soft money through the national effort.

4. Brooks Jackson, "Bush, Dukakis Presidential Campaigns Each Spent More than $100 Million," *Wall Street Journal,* December 12, 1988.

5. Paul Houston, "Big Cash Gifts to Parties Skirt Election Laws," *Los Angeles Times,* October 3, 1988.

6. For an extended analysis of soft money, see Herbert E. Alexander, *Strategies for Election Reform* (Washington, D.C.: Project for Comprehensive Campaign Reform, April 1989), pp. 44–57.

7. Jackson, "Bush, Dukakis Presidential Campaigns Each Spent More Than $100 Million," op. cit.

8. Alexander, *Strategies for Election Reform,* op. cit., p. 11.

9. Richard L. Berke, "Spending Limit Up 14% for Primaries," *New York Times,* February 6, 1988.

10. "Update on Status of Presidential Fund," Federal Election Commission memorandum, May 18, 1990.

11. Federal Election Commission, *FEC Record,* AO 1983–25, February 1984, pp. 4–5.

12. "FEC Update: Robertson Is Penalized for Soliciting Funds Before Declaring Candidacy," *Campaign Practices Reports,* vol. 16, no. 1, January 9, 1989, p. 9.

4

FINANCING SENATE AND HOUSE ELECTIONS: THE IMPETUS FOR CAMPAIGN FINANCE REFORM

The political finance reforms of the early 1970s were meant not only to disclose where the money came from and to put limits on the amounts individuals and groups could give but also to put a ceiling on the amounts of money spent in elections. But the Supreme Court ruled in *Buckley* v. *Valeo* that candidates could be limited in spending only if they accepted a benefit such as public funds, to offset the relinquishment of their right to spend freely in their own behalf. This meant that presidential contests would have ceilings because the law passed in the wake of Watergate provided for public funds raised through a checkoff on the income tax form. However, Senate and House elections were not covered by public funding or expenditure limitations.

In 1988, the trend toward what some have called the "Permanent Congress" continued; few House incumbents faced serious challenge, and those defeated were victims, for the most part, of their own ethical improprieties. A surprising finding in the 1988 data was the number of Senate races that looked like House races: More Senate incumbents, it appears, are beginning to face little-known, inexperienced challengers who are unable to raise substantial campaign money. There are still Senate races of the old style, where both candidates are armed with millions of dollars, producing close races. But the Senate trend is surprising; a number of Senate incumbents in 1988 faced challengers who offered little competition.

In congressional races, challengers were generally unable to raise enough money to provide real competition, and incumbents were able to raise more money from PACs than ever before. Senate general election candidates received 24 percent of their funds from PACs; general election House candidates received 40 percent of their receipts from that source. To raise the $4 million the average Senate winner spent in 1988, almost $13,000 would have to be raised every week of the six-year term.[1]

Whether these findings of lessening competition in both houses of Congress extend into the 1990 elections remains to be seen, but 1992 may well be more competitive, at least in House contests, following reapportionment.

THE CONTROVERSY OVER A TREND TOWARD A "PERMANENT CONGRESS"

The notion of a "Permanent Congress" has been debated recently in the national press. Some House incumbents are quick to point out that there has been an infusion of new blood into the House in the decade of the 1980s. In an article titled "The Permanent Congress Is a Myth," Representative Al Swift (D–WA) wrote, "Members elected since 1980 now have more votes than members elected before 1980."[2] However, most House turnover in recent elections has been due to retirement, death, and redistricting rather than to incumbents being defeated by challengers in a stable district. Some House members retire from that chamber to run for the Senate or for another political office, and others retire for age or health reasons or to make more money as lobbyists or lawyers. Turnover occurs, but the numbers of defeated House incumbents are few, as shown in the following breakdown:

1980	31
1982	29
1984	16
1986	8
1988	6

Swift and others have cited the fact that 244 House members have been replaced in the 1980s.[3] However, most of the defeats took place in 1980 and 1982. The fact that so few incumbents have been defeated since the 1984 elections is some indication that incumbents of both parties are moving beyond the reach of electoral competition. Reelection rates, coupled with the widening gap between incumbent and challenger spending, have led many to discuss the trend toward a "Permanent Congress," regardless of the fact that turnover due to death and retirement continues to bring new members into the House of Representatives.[4]

ANALYZING HOUSE AND SENATE SPENDING DATA: 1988

There are two kinds of Senate and House campaigns. Lumping all into one set of data, mixing well, and reporting statistics obscures what has actually been happening in these races. It is more helpful to view these elections as belonging in two very different categories, "hard fought" and "low key," derived from the research of Mark C. Westlye. His outline of levels of competition in Senate races applies equally to House contests: "In low-key elections, voters are much less familiar with the challenger than the incumbent, and voter defections (voters crossing party lines) favor the incumbent. In hard-fought races, both candidates are well known, and the incumbent has no advantages in defections [from the challenger's partisans]."[5]

If these differences are not taken into account, the spending patterns in the 1988 House and Senate elections seem to tell one kind of story: It appears that spending levels are nearly flat between the 1986 and 1988 cycles. Spending for House races rose only 7.2 percent, and Senate spending actually decreased 5 percent from 1986 levels. One might be tempted to conclude that spending finally was leveling out or even decreasing in House and Senate contests. This would look even more convincing when comparing the 1987–1988 cycle to the large increases in spending found in the previous election cycles, as shown in Table 4.1.

What is to be made of the drop in the increase of expenditures from 1986 to 1988? Observers have known for years that aggregate House spending data is biased by the vast number of challengers who raise and spend very little money. What seems to be new is the number of Senate challengers who are spending one-fifth or less the amount that Senate incumbents spend. Note that House spending went up in 1988 by 7.2 percent, while Senate spending decreased 5 percent. It would appear that the number of hard-fought Senate races decreased in 1988, bringing down the aggregate spending figures. However, hard-fought races were indeed more expensive in 1988 than in 1986. In the November 1988 election, only 4 Senate incumbents and 6 House incumbents were defeated; 1 House member lost in the primary. It is therefore important to look at the increased spending by candidates

TABLE 4.1
Congressional Campaign Expenditures, 1972–1988 (in millions)

Election Cycle	Total	Senate	House
1971–1972	$ 77.3	$ 30.7	$ 46.5
1973–1974	88.2	34.7	53.5
1975–1976	115.5	44.0	71.5
1977–1978	194.8	85.2	109.7
1979–1980	239.0	102.9	136.0
1981–1982	342.4	138.4	204.0
1983–1984	374.1	170.5	203.6
1985–1986	450.9	211.6	239.3
1987–1988	457.0	201.2	256.5

Source: Citizens' Research Foundation compilation, based on FEC and other data.

who won, leaving out the low-spending challengers; then, a clearer picture emerges of the costs of a hard-fought race.

Looking only at the expenditures of winning (mostly incumbent) campaigns, costs increased over the 1986 levels by 18.5 percent for Senate candidates and 10.3 percent for House winners. The average Senate winner spent nearly $4 million in 1988; the average House winner spent nearly $400,000.[6]

There is a steady increase in spending from cycle to cycle among winners, and again that means mostly incumbent spending. As noted before, what is surprising is the increasing number of challengers who expend very little. This flooding of the electoral system with "token challengers" who spend one-fifth or less than opposing incumbents may make aggregate data on Senate and House races suspect for comparative purposes. Neither average costs nor aggregate data can be used with confidence as a yardstick by which to judge the costs of elections; it is clear, though, that most incumbents routinely raise big money, and most challengers raise negligible amounts. It is also clear that not all spending in a two-year House cycle or a six-year Senate cycle is campaign directed. Early spending on polls, consultants, and gearing up may occur a year or more prior to the election, before it is known whether the incumbent will be challenged or how seriously. We will first deal with the problems presented by spending patterns in House races.

TOKEN CHALLENGERS IN HOUSE RACES

In the 1988 elections, with only 7 incumbent defeats (5 of which can be attributed to scandals), House competition hit an all-time low. In

1988, more than 95.8 percent of all incumbents in the House won with 60 percent or more of the vote, safe seats by anyone's definition.[7] In 77 races, incumbents ran without any major party opposition.

Incumbents win because challengers are "obscure, and ill-funded."[8] The 1988 House elections produced the largest crop of invisible "token challengers" since attention was first paid to challenger quality in the 1970s. A "token challenger" is just a name on the ballot; he or she does not raise enough money to go on television or engage in a visible campaign. In 1988, 230 challengers in House races had a median spending figure of less than $50,000. That means that 83 percent of all House challengers were unable to raise enough money to achieve even the most minimal visibility to the electorate.

A good example of the token House challenger can be found in Texas. One of the largest disparities between incumbent and challenger spending in 1988 took place when Congressman Steve Bartlett, representing the third district, spent more than $1 million to defeat a challenger who spent $17,757.

A comparison between the 1984, 1986, and 1988 data shows the downward trend in challenger quality in House races. There was an increase of 24 percent in the number of token House challengers (those who spent $50,000 or less) from 1984 to 1988, pointing to a growing army of challengers who cannot afford to wage a modern campaign: A candidate can buy very little with less than $50,000. One 1984 House challenger in the first congressional district of a rural midwestern state, for example, raised and spent $51,000. That money bought a staff of two, three radio ads written and produced locally, one poll (costs shared with the Senate candidate), and one television spot, locally produced, that was shown fewer than twenty times in the general election. There were three direct mailings, again locally produced, to a select number of key partisans. Overall, the spending was stretched to cover the twenty-seven counties in the district. On election day, the challenger received 26 percent of the vote.

There were only 47 House challengers in the 1988 election cycle who approached or achieved the mean spending of House winners. Of this select group of challengers able to raise more money, the top 5 spenders were responsible for the defeat of incumbents. One successful House challenger won while spending only $385,400. The other 6 won by spending $500,000 or more. And the closer they got to spending $400,000, the closer these challengers came to winning the seat. Of the top 10 spenders for House seats, 2 were challengers—1 won and 1 lost, and each spent in excess of $1.3 million; however, both their winning opponents spent at least $1.4 million. Those who lost with between 41 and 45 percent of the vote spent a median of $355,016.

Those who were even closer, receiving more than 45 percent of the vote, had a median spending figure of $378,469.[9]

SPENDING AND LOSING INCUMBENTS IN THE HOUSE

Even for incumbents who lost in 1988, the more they were able to spend, the closer they came to hanging on to their seats. But even incumbents can spend large sums of money and still not be reelected; money can buy many things, but it might not overcome scandal. And it also is likely that an incumbent who is scared will spend more than one who feels secure. Nevertheless, of the 6 incumbents defeated in 1988, those who spent the most money came closest to winning.

As stated earlier, most House defeats were explainable as the natural result of scandal. Challengers facing such vulnerable incumbents were able to raise, for the most part, an adequate campaign budget. In some interesting cases, the scandal that hurt the incumbent did not surface until late in the election, and for this reason, some 1988 challengers who ordinarily would not have been seen as potential winners walked off with the seat.

St. Germain/Machtley

A good example of this phenomenon occurred in Rhode Island, where House committee chair Ferdinand St. Germain (banking committee) looked like an easy winner. His challenger was described by *Congressional Quarterly* as "an attorney and underfinanced political newcomer" who "was not considered a potent general election threat."[10] Throughout the campaign, there had been an undercurrent of questions concerning favorable treatment of certain banks by St. Germain's committee, particularly hard-pressed savings and loans. But it was not until two weeks before the general election, when the press published an account of a Justice Department letter that spoke of evidence of serious misconduct, that it really looked like the incumbent was doomed. So Ronald Machtley, a 54-year-old lawyer with no previous political experience, was able to spend $385,402 and defeat an established incumbent who spent $801,289 in a vain attempt to keep his seat. Thanks to an incumbent's scandal, the new congressman is the first Republican to represent the first district of Rhode Island in fifty years.[11]

Swindall/Jones

Another victim of scandal was Pat Swindall of Georgia, the owner of a furniture store. As word got out that he was desperate for money to finish a million-dollar mansion, a sting operation was set up. An undercover agent offered to make a loan of $850,000 with money that was supposedly garnered from the drug trade. Swindall accepted this generous loan and was videotaped in the process. In June 1988, the *Atlanta Constitution* broke the story, and Swindall subsequently was indicted. Under indictment, he received the lowest percentage of votes of any incumbent in 1988: 40 percent. Running against an indicted congressman might have helped Ben Jones raise some of his campaign budget of $516,737. Swindall spent $696,301 to get his 40 percent.[12]

Davis/Sangmeister

One incumbent defeat was not the result of any scandal on the part of the incumbent. Jack Davis, of Illinois' fourth district, defended his seat for the first time and lost, having been hastily appointed the Republican nominee in 1986 after the incumbent died. Davis spent $348,339; his opponent, a well-known Democratic state senator, George E. Sangmeister, was able to spend $359,942. The incumbent lost by barely 1,000 votes.[13]

Lowey/DioGuardi

New York's twentieth district provided the year's only victory for a female challenger. The winner, Democrat Nita Lowey, was able to do something few challengers have been able to do: She spent more than $1.3 million to win her seat ($1,309,873).[14] The incumbent, Joseph DioGuardi, had won narrowly in an open-seat race in 1984, garnering 50 percent of the vote. Before DioGuardi, the twentieth district had been represented for sixteen years by a liberal Democrat, Dick Ottinger.

This district includes a large part of Westchester County, in one of the most expensive media markets in the nation. Nita Lowey was a former assistant secretary of state for New York, with strong ties to Mario Cuomo. The fact that she was able to spend more than $1 million certainly contributed to her win; nevertheless, a scandal late in the campaign undoubtedly helped her eke out a 5,000-vote victory.

DioGuardi had been hit by charges that a car dealer had promised to reimburse his employees for giving the maximum individual contribution to DioGuardi's campaign. Because this car dealer also was actively involved in the incumbent's campaign, it looked like a sweetheart deal that the congressman—a CPA who campaigned on his attention to financial details—either knew about or should have known about. But even with that taint of scandal, DioGuardi spent $1,567,129 and came within a few thousand votes of retaining his seat.[15]

Chappell/Jones

The 1988 defeat of twenty-year House veteran Bill Chappell, Jr., was termed "the biggest upset in any of the nation's 435 districts."[16] Chappell had been unopposed in previous elections in Florida's fifth congressional district, but in 1987, he was widely reported to be a target of investigators in the Pentagon procurement scandal. It was disclosed that in his 1983 income tax he deducted $30,000 in rent to a company he owned, which then promptly lent him the money. He also sold a failed health spa he owned to a subsidiary of Martin Marietta for $195,000 in 1986, although he was chair of the Defense Appropriations Subcommittee at the time. In addition, his campaign raised more than $250,000 from defense-related PACs and individuals.[17]

Analyzing his victory, the new congressman, Craig T. James, who won by 791 votes, said that Bill Chappell had "beat himself."[18] Chappell had spent $1,069,699 to lose by the slimmest of margins to a reformer who spent $313,415, none of it from PACs.

Sweeney/Laughlin

Freshman Congressman Mac Sweeney of Texas's fourteenth congressional district lost when his opponent pointed out the glaring discrepancies between his campaign literature and the facts of his life. "His 1984 campaign literature highlighted his time at the University of Texas Law School, and said his work had been published in the Law Review. But according to *Texas Monthly,* he dropped out of law school and never had anything published in the Review."[19]

Sweeney's spending in 1988 was $645,988, but it was not enough to protect him from charges made during the campaign that he claimed to cosponsor bills he had not touched. The challenger, Gregory H. Laughlin, won with 53 percent, spending $600,114.[20]

Konnyu/Campbell

The only incumbent to lose in a primary election in 1988 was Ernest Konnyu, a Hungarian-American whose family had emigrated to the United States to flee communism. Konnyu had embarrassed former Congressman Ed Zschau so much by his unorthodox behavior in his first term that Zschau turned against him in 1988. The former congressman enlisted the help of the wealthiest man in the district, high-tech billionaire David Packard, and they joined forces behind a primary challenger, Tom Campbell.

The *Almanac of American Politics* called Konnyu "an excitable man, who had the highest staff turnover of any congressman in 1987."[21] Then the *San Jose Mercury News* reported that Konnyu had made "unwelcome sexual remarks to a female aide."[22]

The main conclusion to be drawn about the losing incumbents in the 1988 election is that most members of Congress are in safe seats. Most do not engage in sexual abuse in office, and certainly most would not be likely to accept "drug money" from an undercover FBI agent. The few caught in scandal draw well-financed and—if the scandal is publicized in advance of the deadline for candidates to file—well-qualified challengers. However, one lesson of 1988 was that a few challengers who started out as token candidates ended up as representatives; these were people who had never before run for any public office, and more experienced public servants had earlier rejected the opportunity to run for Congress, assuming that it would be a hopeless task.

The fact that Swindall and St. Germain, among others, came so close to retaining their seats might be attributable to the vast amounts of money they were able to spend. It is hard to sort out, and causality in politics is a slippery issue. Nevertheless, the question should be posed: Will people identified with scandals be able to fend off challengers in the future by spending large sums of money? And are those identified with sex scandals thought of differently? The small win margins of challengers defeating scandal-ridden incumbents warrants further research.

THE 1988 SENATE DATA:
THE RISE OF THE TOKEN SENATE CHALLENGER

Although House incumbents were able to build a so-called "Permanent Congress" in the 1970s and 1980s by amassing campaign war chests that convinced experienced politicians they would be foolish to run against them, Senate races were still being hotly contested. As Richard S. Beth wrote in 1984: "The contrast with Senate races is instructive. Incumbents [in the Senate] possess no similar electoral advantage [compared to safe House incumbents], though their perquisites are similar. There is less gap in campaign budgets, awareness levels, and contact rates [between incumbent and challengers]."[23] However, in 1988, total Senate incumbent spending was $101 million; total challenger spending was marginally more than half that amount, $55.9 million.

In 1978, the National Election Study done at the University of Michigan first asked a sample of voters across the country if they could recognize the names of the incumbents and challengers in House and Senate races. The results showed clearly that voters were familiar with well-funded incumbents in both the House and Senate; they also were familiar with the usually well-funded open-seat candidates. But fewer than half of those surveyed could recognize the names of the poorly funded House challengers. Senate challengers, who were raising and spending nearly equal amounts in the 1970s, were nearly as well known as Senate incumbents, as shown in Table 4.2.

This situation produced close Senate races in the 1970s. In that decade, 54.6 percent of incumbents received between 55 and 59 percent of the vote, but only 37.3 percent of incumbents got more than 60 percent of the vote. Thus, most Senate incumbents did not cut such an imposing electoral figure that they could deter potential challengers with their previous large victory margins. In electoral analysis, only the 37.3 percent who garnered 60 percent or more of the vote could consider themselves as having a "safe seat" in the Senate.[24]

However, this pattern changed in 1988; only 9 percent of winning Senate incumbents won by less than 60 percent of the vote. Some 53 percent won by 60 percent or better, and 38 percent won by a margin often described as a "landslide," receiving 64 percent or more.[25] These superincumbents included superstars, such as George Mitchell of Maine (who received 81 percent of the vote), as well as lesser-known figures of little national celebrity, such as the late Spark Matsunaga of Hawaii (receiving 76.6 percent of the vote).[26] What these extraordinarily safe Senate incumbents had in common was one thing only: they outspent their challengers by factors of four to twenty times.

They were able to do so not because they spent more than the average for a Senate incumbent; in fact, they spent far less. Rather, these incumbents all faced ill-funded and, in many cases, inexperienced challengers who offered them no competition or incentive to spend more heavily. The problem was not incumbent spending; it was the inability of Senate challengers to raise enough money to challenge effectively.

The story does not lie in the aggregate figures, which average out to a little more than twice as much spending by incumbents; the story

TABLE 4.2
Candidate Recognition in Contested Races: House and Senate, 1978

House incumbents	93 percent
Senate incumbents	96 percent
House challengers	44 percent
Senate challengers	86 percent
Open-seat candidates	72 percent
Open-seat candidates	88 percent

Source: Thomas E. Mann and Raymond E. Wolfinger, "Candidates and Parties in Congressional Elections," *American Political Science Review,* vol. 74, 1980, table 4, p. 623. Reprinted with permission.

TABLE 4.3
Senate Incumbent Spending as Factored Against Challenger Spending

Incumbent Spending			
2 times challenger	3 times challenger	4 times challenger	5 times challenger
Burdick	Wallop	Danforth	Sasser
Sarbanes	Bingaman		Kennedy
P. Wilson	Durenberger		
6 times challenger	9–12 times challenger	20 times challenger	
Bentsen	Byrd	Hatch	
Moynihan	Heinz		
Riegle	Mitchell		
	Lugar		
	Matsunaga		
	DeConcini		

Incumbent and Challenger Spending Virtually Equal Amounts
Weicker (defeated)
Roth (challenger spent $233,199 more)
Melcher (defeated)
Hecht (defeated)
Lautenberg (won with 52 percent)
Metzenbaum (won with 56 percent)
Chafee (won with 54 percent)

1988 open seats: Florida, Mississippi, Vermont, Virginia, Washington, Wisconsin, and Nebraska (where the incumbent, David Karnes, had been appointed a few months before the campaign began to fill the seat of the late Ed Zorinsky; thus, the dynamics of the race more closely resembled an open-seat election).

Source: Calculations from FEC data.

is in the individual races that were affected by the disparity in spending between incumbent and challenger, as shown in Table 4.3. This disparity also showed up at the polls in huge victories for incumbents. The 10 incumbent senators who won with 64 percent or more of the vote include:

	Percent
Robert Byrd (WV)	64
Edward Kennedy (MA)	64
Jim Sasser (TN)	65
John Heinz (PA)	66
John Danforth (MO)	67
Daniel Moynihan (NY)	67
Orrin Hatch (UT)	67

James Jeffords (VT)	68
Spark Matsunaga (HI)	77
George Mitchell (ME)	81

Token Challengers for the Senate

In 1988, almost half of all Senate incumbents spent five times or more than their challengers. This phenomenon was found in both large and small states and for incumbents who were both Democrats and Republicans. Because their challengers raised so little money, the incumbents could, without effort, spend five, ten, or, in the case of Orrin Hatch, twenty times the amount spent by their challengers. One might assume that token challengers would be found in races against powerful incumbents with national reputations, where it would be hard to find an opponent eager to take them on. Such was the case in some contests where spending was lopsided. Yet, some candidates without national reputations also managed to rack up large win margins against token opposition, including some Democrats who were likely targets for Republicans aiming to retake the Senate. Following are a few illustrations of the token Senate challengers.

The Senate Challenger with the Smallest Campaign Spending

Matsunaga/Hustace

Spark M. Matsunaga, senator from Hawaii, faced a little-known, 70-year-old rancher from Molokai without much campaign experience. Challenger Maria M. Hustace spent the smallest amount of any Senate challenger—only $33,325. Yet, Senator Matsunaga spent $494,580 to defeat Hustace.[27]

The Senator Who Spent Twenty Times His Challenger

Hatch/Moss

Matsunaga was little known outside Hawaii and the mainland Japanese-American community. In contrast, Utah's Orrin Hatch is a national figure, a man out front on various conservative issues. And Utah is now the most Republican state in the nation. Yet, Hatch spent $3,706,381; his opponent was able to spend only $153,475.[28] Why did Hatch spend almost as much money as he spent in 1982 (when his challenger was a popular former mayor of the state's largest city) against what was obviously token opposition in 1988? Why did he spend so much in a low-population (three House members), inexpensive media market state like Utah? Are senators spending money just because it is available? Clearly, many individuals and PACs are giving money to senators early on, before they know whether they face a serious challenger or an unknown. And even when it is apparent the incumbent is in no electoral difficulty, PAC money is still readily available to incumbents.

Senators Rack Up Record Win Margins Against Low-Spending Challengers

Mitchell/Wyman

George Mitchell received 81 percent of the vote in 1988. Did the fact that he spent ten times as much as his challenger have anything to do with this impressive victory? Or did money have a more indirect effect, discouraging serious politicians from challenging the former head of the Democratic Senate Campaign Committee, leaving Mitchell to face so underfunded a challenger that even moderate spending would be five or ten times the challenger's budget? Mitchell's 1988 challenger was a "religious conservative activist" at the far-right fringe of the Republican party.[29] It could be argued that it was the weakness of the challenger that was the deciding factor in giving Mitchell the greatest victory in the history of Maine Senate campaigns.

Jasper S. Wyman was the hapless challenger. He was able to spend only $147,760, although Mitchell spent $1,471,426.[30] Maine politicians reportedly knew that Mitchell was not in any electoral danger in 1988. Yet, he spent more than $1.4 million in the low-population state of Maine to defeat an underfunded fundamentalist. Perhaps $1 million is the minimum amount any serious candidate would spend for a Senate race, regardless of the size of the state or the quality of the challenger. But large win margins seem to come as much from challenger weakness as incumbent virtue. And the biggest challenger weakness is the inability to raise money, allowing the incumbent to outspend by factors of ten or more.

Lugar/Wickes

Richard Lugar was another incumbent who made history in 1988. He won 68 percent of the vote, breaking the previous record win margin of Dan Quayle (61 percent in 1986). The fact that his challenger was "an underfinanced Democrat who never got any ads on the air" may have had something to do with it.[31] Lugar's win is all the more impressive when one considers he won in ninety-one out of ninety-two counties, "all but eight of them with more than 60 percent of the vote."[32]

Lugar's 1988 challenger, Jack Wickes, spent what was perhaps a respectable amount of money for a House race ($314,233), but because of the size of Indiana and the necessity of buying television time in the Chicago and Cincinnati markets, much more was needed to do well statewide.[33] One can speculate on the effect a 68 percent win margin will have on any potential challenger to Lugar should he decide to run again in 1994.

Moynihan/McMillan

Daniel Patrick Moynihan won 67 percent of the vote, breaking all previous records for New York Senate races. He carried every county in the state except one and, along with the California incumbents, holds the distinction of having won the highest number of votes in U.S. Senate electoral history. Moynihan spent $4,809,810; his little-known opponent, Robert R. McMillan, spent $528,989.[34]

Spending and Senators Targeted for Defeat

The National Republican Senatorial Committee, chaired by Senator Rudy Boschwitz of Minnesota, had targeted several senators for defeat in 1988.[35] Even in cases where the Republicans were targeting incumbents, some challengers failed to raise a competitive war chest and seemed to be token challengers.

Bingaman/Valentine

Jeff Bingaman, first elected a senator from New Mexico in the low-turnout year of 1982, was targeted by the GOP. But Bingaman drew a weak challenger. In 1982, when spending between incumbent Harrison Schmidt and Bingaman was almost dead even, Bingaman won with 54 percent. In 1988, the challenger, Bill Valentine, was only able to spend $659,624, against Bingaman's $2,808,659. Although he was targeted for defeat, Bingaman was able to post the best win margin of a Democratic Senate campaign in New Mexico since 1960 (with 63 percent of the vote).[36]

The Republicans also targeted Quentin Burdick of North Dakota, Howard Metzenbaum of Ohio, and John Melcher of Montana. Burdick, at age 80, outspent his challenger by a 2 to 1 margin. Metzenbaum drew a big-spending challenger but still won with an impressive margin. Melcher was the only one to be defeated.

Melcher/Burns

Melcher and his challenger spent almost the same amount of money, $1.3 million, and the challenger won with 52 percent of the vote.[37] Melcher had previously been targeted by the National Conservative Political Action Committee (NCPAC) in 1982 and held on with 54 percent of the vote. A local veterinarian, he had been able to stave off conservative attacks in 1982 by making the challenger look like the recipient of help from unpopular outsiders. The 1988 Republican challenger was a farm-news broadcaster, a Montanan named Conrad Burns.

Metzenbaum/Voinovich

The case of Howard Metzenbaum clearly shows the escalating costs of winning Senate campaigns: In 1982, he spent $2,794,172 against a challenger who spent $1,025,595, and he won with 57 percent of the vote. In 1988, Metzenbaum won with an identical 57 percent, but this time, he spent $8,547,545. His challenger, George Voinovich, former mayor of Cleveland, spent $8,233,859.[38] Despite the challenger's ability to raise substantial sums of money, he failed to unseat this targeted Democratic incumbent.

What is to be made of the number of token challengers in Senate races, those who are outspent by the incumbents by ratios of 3, 6, and 9 to 1? (Orrin Hatch even outspent his challenger by 20 to 1.) Is it a matter of a discouragement effect, a giving up in the next cycle after a tough race was lost in 1982? In 1988, the average winning Senate campaign cost more than $4 million.[39] But many Senate challengers in 1988 failed to raise even one-third that amount.

PARALLELS BETWEEN TOKEN
HOUSE AND SENATE CHALLENGERS

An interesting parallel exists between House races in the 1970s and Senate races in the 1980s. As House incumbents began spending more money on their campaigns, the gap between incumbent and challenger spending widened. The gap gave a $16,523 advantage to the incumbent in 1974. By 1984, the gap grew to $117,050. It reached an all-time high of $264,104 in 1988, more than double the previous incumbent-challenger spending gap.[40] "In fact, the average major-party House challenger in 1988 spent less than the average challenger spent in 1980."[41] As the spending gap has widened, House incumbents have become more electorally secure, so that virtually the only way to lose is to be caught in a major scandal. Turnover instead comes through retirements, deaths, and decisions to run for other offices.

There was a spiraling increase in the costs of running for the House in the 1970s. As costs increased, the gap between incumbents, who could foot the bill, and challengers, who were unable to raise larger and larger sums of money, also increased. Incumbents started to face more first-time candidates, who were inexperienced and unable to raise money; win margins against such "invisible opponents" increased. And as incumbent win margins increased, rational politicians were deterred from entering a race as a challenger to a sitting member of the House. Now, more token candidates run, win margins soar, and the cycle feeds on itself, producing greater and greater incumbent security.

In the House, the spiral feeds itself quickly, as incumbents are up for reelection every two years. In the Senate, the spiral has been slower to build and harder to discern, as there were still years when a few incumbents faced tough challengers and lost, such as 1986. The challenge for the political parties is to take measures to fund challengers better or to press the Congress to enact some type of campaign finance reform that will improve electoral competition.

DEEP POCKETS IN THE 1988 SENATE ELECTIONS

The Supreme Court decision in *Buckley* v. *Valeo* enshrined the idea that the spending of one's own money cannot be limited outright; money spent on a political career is money acting as a personal political voice. Therefore, such personal spending cannot be controlled unless public funding is provided by the government and accepted by the candidate. If there had been a limit on personal contributions, as has been proposed in some versions of political finance reform legislation, the 27 percent of Senate races where more than $100,000 was provided through "self-financing" in 1988 would have been most directly affected. Of the 9 such candidates, 3 won, as shown in Table 4.4, and only Frank Lautenberg was an incumbent.

It is interesting to note that all the winning Senate candidates who spent more than $100,000 of their own money also topped the list for the largest campaign debts among winners.[42] The combination of deep pockets and campaign debts is not new to Senate races; there were still 27 Senate winners who spent little or no personal money on their campaigns in 1988. Some lend their campaigns money and then write off the loans as contributions.

The Kohl Case

A good deal of media attention in 1988 was focused on the Senate race in Wisconsin, where Herbert H. Kohl, a multimillionaire, made

TABLE 4.4
Senate Candidates Who Spent $100,000 or More of Their Own Money

Name	State	Personal Funds	Vote Percent
Herbert Kohl	WI	$6,920,071	52.1
Peter Dawkins	NJ	736,290	45.2
Frank Lautenberg	NJ	301,500	53.6
James Dunn	MI	250,808	38.5
William Valentine	NM	232,135	36.7
S. B. Woo	DE	160,000	37.9
Richard Licht	RI	149,620	45.4
Robert McMillan	NY	118,060	31.1
Robert Kerrey	NE	102,500	56.7

Source: Larry Makinson, "The Price of Admission: An Illustrated Atlas of Spending in the 1988 Congressional Elections," Center for Responsive Politics, Washington, D.C., 1989, p. 21. Reprinted with permission.

a public virtue of his ability to fund his campaign almost entirely out of his own fortune. Senator Kohl was the only 1988 winner to refuse all PAC money.[43]

Kohl's case showed the ability of money to edge political experience out of a Senate race. The prospect of an open seat when Senator William Proxmire retired attracted the interest of several sitting House members, including Congressman Jim Moody. Moody was a former professor of political science at the University of Wisconsin, with a lifetime of public service. He entered the 1988 Senate race in 1987 but got out when it became clear that he could not raise as much money as Kohl could spend.[44]

Kohl, the new junior senator from Wisconsin, had built up the family supermarket business and became a local celebrity as the owner of the Milwaukee Bucks basketball team. He spent close to $7 million of his own money to win his Senate seat.[45]

Not all candidates were deterred by Kohl's willingness to support his ambition with his own money. In the Democratic primary, he faced a former governor, Tony Earl, who also had "a statewide network of supporters."[46] Earl portrayed Kohl as a man who did not know much about the issues but was going to spend whatever it took to ensure his election. In the end, Earl only received 38 percent of the vote. Thus, a former governor and a congressman were bested by a political newcomer.

In the general election, Kohl spent $500,000 more than the challenger, State Senator Susan Engeleiter, to win with 52 percent of the vote. One of a few Senate candidates in 1988 to openly campaign against PAC money, Kohl's slogan was "Nobody's Senator but Yours."[47] He incurred the second largest campaign debt among Senate candidates, at $796,157.[48]

Lautenberg/Dawkins

There were 8 other candidates who spent more than $100,000 of their own money to run for the Senate in 1988.[49] Only 1 of these was an incumbent—Frank Lautenberg of New Jersey. In the 1982 elections, he spent $5 million of his own money to beat Congresswoman Millicent Fenwick, winning 51 percent to her 48 percent.[50] Partly because his 1982 margin was so slender, Lautenberg drew a tough Republican challenger in 1988. The Frank Lautenberg-Peter Dawkins contest pitted one self-financed candidate against another. The $736,290 donated by Dawkins to his campaign was the second largest personal contribution of 1988. Third highest was Lautenberg's own, at $301,500.[51]

In 1988, those willing to spend their own money also were among the most willing to go into debt. Whenever Dawkins was running out of cash, "Lautenberg always had reserves,"[52] perhaps because he was willing to incur the largest campaign debt of 1988—$3,718,854.[53] He also received the fourth largest amount of PAC funds among Senate candidates, with $1,631,341.[54] He won with 54 percent of the vote. This was one of the few seats where the Republicans had pinned their hopes of regaining Senate control, but the Democratic incumbent won with his own money, considerable PAC donations, and considerable debt.

Riegle/Dunn

Fourth on the list was Jim Dunn, one of the 7 big-spending Senate challengers. Dunn's case is particularly notable because he is the first candidate attempting to sue the Republican Senatorial Campaign Committee for breach of promise, claiming that he never saw the substantial donations he was led to believe would appear.[55]

Dunn was attempting to unseat Senator Donald Riegle. Riegle, chair of the Senate banking committee, only spent a portion of his campaign war chest defeating Dunn. At the end of the 1988 campaign, after spending $3,383,849, the incumbent had $855,659 left over.[56]

DEEP POCKETS AND CANDIDATE RECRUITMENT

The Kerrey Case

Robert Kerrey, who spent $102,500 of his own money, ran one of the most interesting races in the 1988 cycle, as well as a race that helped cement the Democratic control of the Senate. It describes, in a way, one kind of interaction between money and politics that has not received much attention. Much has been said on the subject of the corrupting influence of special interest and PAC money on our politicians. But less has been said on the way citizens who have financial resources are recruited to run for office not because of their previous experience in politics but because they can help finance the campaign.

As costs spiral, there could be a trend toward a two-tier system of politics: competitive races, where incumbents are challenged by the wealthy, and noncompetitive races, where the challenger is a token.

Kerrey owned a restaurant business in Nebraska. He had dabbled a bit in politics as a member of Vietnam Veterans Against the War. But Kerrey had been Nebraska's Congressional Medal of Honor winner and had lost his right foot in the war. *The Almanac of American Politics* describes Kerrey as a "political unknown" in 1982 when he defeated Republican Governor Charles Thone. What the *Almanac* does not report is that, according to some sources, Kerrey was recruited to run by Senator J. James Exon in large part because he had money and no other Democrat wanted to try to unseat a sitting Republican governor in one of the most Republican states in the union. Some say that Kerrey was originally recruited to run for mayor of Lincoln and that it was his own decision to enter his first political race as a candidate for governor. In either case, most local sources agree it was largely Kerrey's ability to finance his own campaign that made him attractive to the financially strapped Nebraska Democratic party.[57] When he ran for governor, Kerrey learned the advantage personal wealth could hold. In the last days of the 1982 campaign, he was able to borrow thousands of dollars to put ads on television, and after he won, he held a series of fund-raisers to retire the debt. He applied the same formula to his 1988 Senate campaign, running up the fifth largest campaign debt of the season.[58]

Clearly, then, the ability of the candidate to fund part of his or her own campaign can affect candidate recruitment, discourage other candidates from attempting a challenge, and even, as in the case of Senator Kohl, allow the candidate to remain free of all PAC money. Any change in regulations regarding personal contributions would have repercussions in all these areas.

PAC SPENDING IN HOUSE AND SENATE RACES

The big news in 1988 was the shift in giving by business PACs. In 1982, Republican candidates were seen as the natural recipients of business PAC money, just as the Democrats were the natural recipients of money from labor PACs. This dovetailed nicely with the ideas of political theorists who saw interest groups as representing the public interest writ large. As long as PACs gave along ideological lines and represented differing ideologies, PAC giving was considered to be just another expression of pluralist democracy. But PACs have tended to move away from ideology and instead have become incumbent-oriented.

Tony Coelho, chair of the Democratic Congressional Campaign Committee in the early 1980s, used a certain logic when persuading traditionally conservative PACs to support Democratic incumbents: It is better to have access to a sitting member of the House than to waste money on a challenger who is likely to lose. Coelho's campaign worked, and by 1988, a record 55 percent of business PAC money was funneled to Democrats, almost exclusively incumbents. Just six years before, Republican candidates garnered 60 percent of business PAC dollars.[59]

Three out of every four PAC dollars in 1988 went to incumbents of both parties, representing an increase of 6 percent over the percentage given to 1986 incumbents. Proportionately, challengers got even fewer dollars in 1988: The percentage of PAC dollars for challengers declined from 14.2 percent in 1986 to just 11.8 percent in 1988, an all-time low.[60] The remaining PAC money went to open seats. Although the percentage of PAC dollars declined in such races from 17 percent in 1986 to 14 percent in 1988, there were fewer open seats in 1988.[61]

In keeping with the trend toward funding incumbents and also giving money to committee chairs, House Democrats received $68.4 million from PACs in 1988, a substantial 22 percent increase over the 1986 figure. Senate Democratic candidates received 25 percent more PAC money than in 1986, for a total of $28.4 million.[62]

The Republican candidates clearly were losing the PAC race in 1988. Senate Republican candidates actually received less money in that year than in 1986, perhaps reflecting the difficulty some felt Republicans would have in recapturing the Senate. These candidates raised $23.4

TABLE 4.5
Senate Candidates Who Received More than Half Their Funds from PACs

Name	Party	State	PAC Percentage	PAC Receipts	Won/Lost
James M. Jeffords	Rep.	VT	69.6	$ 679,393	Won
Robert C. Byrd	Dem.	WV	66.4	1,021,570	Won
John Melcher	Dem.	MT	65.6	966,286	Lost
Malcolm Wallop	Rep.	WY	57.6	922,122	Won
Quentin Burdick	Dem.	ND	57.5	1,186,056	Won

Source: Larry Makinson, "The Price of Admission: An Illustrated Atlas of Spending in the 1988 Congressional Elections," Center for Responsive Politics, Washington, D.C., 1989, p. 23. Reprinted with permission.

million from PACs in 1988, down from $27.5 million in 1986. House Republican candidates, on the other hand, raised a bit more PAC money in 1988: $35.7 million, compared with $33.5 million in 1986.[63]

PAC money has always been less important in Senate races. Of 33 Senate winners, only 5 raised 50 percent or more of their moneys from PACs, as shown in Table 4.5.[64] All were from low-population states. To a large degree, those who spend less than the average for reelection have the largest percentage of PAC money. Counting full six-year terms, 20 senate candidates raised $1 million or more from PACs—17 incumbents, 1 challenger, and 2 open-seat candidates.[65]

The average Senate winner was able to raise a little more than $1 million from PACs in 1988, and 6 were able to get considerably more. Those who received in excess of $1.5 million were:

Lloyd Bentsen	TX	$2,617,311
Pete Wilson	CA	$2,400,342
David Durenberger	MN	$1,791,146
Frank Lautenberg	NJ	$1,631,341
James Sasser	TN	$1,620,300
Donald Riegle	MI	$1,536,168

Source: Larry Makinson, "The Price of Admissions: An Illustrated Atlas of Spending in the 1988 Congressional Elections," Center for Responsive Politics, Washington, D.C., 1989, p. 23.

All 6 were winners, and only Wilson (in the most expensive Senate race of 1988 and as the top Senate spender at nearly $13 million) and Lautenberg won with less than 55 percent of the vote. Many of these senators knew from the beginning of the campaign that their seats were safe for they were running against little-known challengers. In the end, they all won handily; Riegle got 60 percent of the vote, Sasser had 65 percent, Durenberger got 56 percent, and Bentsen, running as both vice presidential candidate and senator in Texas, received 59 percent.[66]

Of these top 6, both Durenberger and Riegle became involved in ethics charges after the campaigns were over. Riegle is one of the "Keating Five," discussed in Chapter 5. Durenberger was charged with several improprieties, including renting an apartment from his own company and paying the rent with campaign funds. In July 1990, he was reprimanded by the Senate.[67]

PAC money is now the key to House campaigns, as Table 4.6 shows.

In House races, 210 of the 435 winners owed half or more of their campaign treasuries to PACs. Considering that 31 House incumbents won reelection by spending less than $100,000 and that there were 26

TABLE 4.6
Percentage of House Campaign Funds from PACs by Party

	Less than 30%	30–50%	50–70%	Over 70%
Democrats	19 seats	82	124	35
Republicans	34 seats	90	46	5

Source: Derived from Larry Makinson, "The Price of Admission: An Illustrated Atlas of Spending in the 1988 Congressional Elections," Center for Responsive Politics, Washington, D.C., 1989, p. 34.

open-seat winners, 56 percent of all incumbents spending $100,000 or more got at least half their money from PACs.[68]

Given the role PACs have played in campaign financing in the 1980s, it is difficult to imagine American politics without PACs. Yet, legislation passed in the Senate in 1990 proposed their elimination. There are those who describe PACs as a means of citizen participation in the electoral process, wherein those with small donations can, by aggregating their contributions with others, have a voice in the political system once reserved for big givers. Others have argued that PAC funds are injecting the voice of special interests into legislative bodies in such a manner that the voices of the unorganized many are drowned out by those of a relatively few interest groups. This debate will likely continue, with the 1988 PAC figures used as evidence by both sides, until a new campaign finance bill is passed and signed into law.

NOTES

1. Larry Makinson, "The Price of Admission: An Illustrated Atlas of Spending in the 1988 Congressional Elections," Center for Responsive Politics, Washington, D.C., 1989, p. 23.
2. Representative Al Swift (D–WA), "The 'Permanent Congress' Is a Myth," Washington Post National Weekly Edition, June 26–July 2, 1989.
3. Also see Representative Mickey Edwards (R–OK), "What 'Permanent Congress'?" New York Times, January 5, 1990; for a Senate perspective, see Alan J. Dixon, "The Power of Incumbency Is a Myth," New York Times, June 12, 1990.
4. Robin Toner, "Are Incumbents Playing with a Stacked Deck?" New York Times, February 7, 1990.
5. Mark C. Westlye, "Competitiveness of Senate Seats and Voting Behavior in Senate Elections," American Journal of Political Science, vol. 27, May 1983, p. 253.
6. "FEC Final Report on 1988 Congressional Campaigns Shows $459 Million Spent," FEC, press release, October 31, 1989, p. 2.
7. Congressional Quarterly Almanac, 1988, vol. 44 (Washington, D.C.: Congressional Quarterly, Inc., 1989), p. 14-A.

8. Richard S. Beth, "Recent Research on Incumbency Advantage in House Elections: Part II," *Congress and the Presidency,* vol. 2, Autumn 1984, p. 211.

9. "FEC Final Report," op. cit., p. 10; also Makinson, op. cit., p. 33.

10. *Congressional Quarterly Almanac, 1988,* op. cit., p. 15–A.

11. Michael Barone and Grant Ujifusa, *The Almanac of American Politics, 1990* (Washington, D.C.: National Journal, 1989), p. 304.

12. Ibid., p. 305.

13. Ibid., p. 357.

14. Ibid., p. 855.

15. Ibid.

16. Ibid., p. 257.

17. Ibid.

18. Ibid.

19. Michael Barone and Grant Ujifusa, *The Almanac of American Politics, 1988* (Washington, D.C.: National Journal, 1987), p. 1166.

20. Barone and Ujifusa, *The Almanac of American Politics, 1990,* op. cit., p. 1193.

21. Ibid., p. 111.

22. Ibid.

23. Beth, op. cit., p. 211.

24. Calculated from FEC data.

25. Ibid.

26. Makinson, op. cit., p. 19.

27. Barone and Ujifusa, *The Almanac of American Politics, 1990,* op. cit., p. 328.

28. Ibid., p. 1228.

29. Ibid., p. 516.

30. Ibid., p. 521.

31. Ibid., p. 399.

32. Ibid.

33. Ibid., p. 402.

34. Ibid., p. 809.

35. *Congressional Quarterly Almanac, 1988,* op. cit., p. 10–A.

36. Barone and Ujifusa, *The Almanac of American Politics, 1990,* op. cit., p. 787.

37. Ibid., p. 707.

38. Ibid., p. 935.

39. Makinson, op. cit., p. 21.

40. Ibid., p. 11.

41. Ibid.

42. Ibid., p. 21–23.

43. Ibid.

44. Barone and Ujifusa, *The Almanac of American Politics, 1990,* op. cit., p. 1315.

45. Makinson, op. cit., p. 21.

46. Ibid.

47. Ibid.

48. Ibid., p. 23.

49. Ibid., p. 21.

50. Barone and Ujifusa, *The Almanac of American Politics, 1990,* op. cit.,
p. 746.

51. Makinson, op. cit., p. 21.

52. Barone and Ujifusa, *The Almanac of American Politics, 1990,* p. 746.

53. Makinson, op. cit., p. 23.

54. Ibid.

55. Barone and Ujifusa, *The Almanac of American Politics, 1990,* op. cit.,
p. 588.

56. Makinson, op. cit., p. 23.

57. Coauthor interviews with Nebraska political leaders, 1984–1990.

58. Makinson, op. cit., p. 23.

59. Ibid., p. 15.

60. "FEC Final Report," op. cit., p. 1.

61. Ibid., p. 2.

62. Ibid.

63. Ibid.

64. Makinson, op. cit., p. 23.

65. "The Winning Edge," *Common Cause News,* Washington, D.C., March
2, 1989, p. 5.

66. Makinson, op. cit., p. 23.

67. Richard L. Berke, "Fellow Senators Vote to Denounce Durenberger,
96–0," *New York Times,* July 26, 1990.

68. Calculations from FEC data.

$ 5
RELATED FINANCING

This chapter covers related or peripheral kinds of financing for presidential and congressional campaigns, by means of soft money and independent expenditures. The two sections below deal with these topics as complementary or supplementary funding in the 1988 elections.

THE CONTROVERSY OVER "SOFT MONEY" IN THE 1988 ELECTIONS

Soft money was much in the news in 1988 because of the highly visible, widely reported competition for such dollars on behalf of the presidential campaigns. Soft money refers to funds that are raised from sources outside the restraints of federal law but spent on activities intended to affect federal election outcomes. By contrast, "hard money" is raised, spent, and publicly disclosed under federal supervision. Some have called the use of soft money a healthy development because it has spurred citizen participation and helped to revitalize state and local party committees. But in the wake of the disclosure that large amounts of soft money were used in the presidential campaigns and that soft money was given by a leading figure in the savings and loan scandal, others have called for federal regulation or even the complete prohibition of such donations.

The 1979 amendments exempt three types of state and local party committee activity from the FECA's contribution and expenditure limits:

74

- State and local party committees may prepare and distribute—including distribution by direct mail—slate cards, sample ballots, palm cards, or other printed listings of three or more candidates for any public office for which an election is held in a given state. None of the candidate listings mentioned, however, may be displayed by such means of general public political advertising as broadcast, newspaper, magazine, or billboard media.
- State and local party committees may pay for grass-roots campaign materials, such as pins, bumper stickers, handbills, brochures, posters, yard signs, and party tabloids or newspapers. These may be used only in connection with volunteer activities and may not be purchased by national party committees and delivered to the local committees or paid for by funds donated by the national committees to the local committees for that purpose. Nor may funds designated by donors for particular federal candidates be used to purchase such materials.
- State and local party committees may conduct voter registration and turnout drives on behalf of their parties' presidential and vice presidential nominees, including the use of telephone banks operated by volunteers, even if paid professionals develop the telephone bank system and phoning instructions and train supervisors. If party candidates for the U.S. House or Senate are mentioned in such drives in more than an incidental way, the costs of the drives allocable to those candidates must be counted as contributions to them. As in the case of volunteer-oriented campaign materials, state and local party committee voter drives may not involve the use of general public political advertising nor may the drives be paid for by funds donated by national party committees or designated by donors for particular candidates.

In all three types of exempted activity, only the portion of the costs allocable to federal candidates must be paid with "hard money," that is, from contributions subject to the limitations and prohibitions of the FECA. The remainder may be paid from funds raised under applicable state laws, which often permit corporate and/or labor union political contributions and give freer rein to individual and PAC contributions than federal law does.[1]

In 1988, both parties at the national level sought soft money contributions to supplement the public funds each presidential and vice presidential ticket received. They were raised not by the parties directly but by the same Bush and Dukakis finance people who raised the candidates' prenomination funds. And much of them were raised in the form of large individual contributions. Some 267 Bush backers gave

$100,000 or more, and some 130 Dukakis supporters gave or were responsible for raising $100,000 each.

Soft money was sanctioned by the 1979 amendments to the Federal Election Campaign Act and is therefore not a loophole, as some have suggested, but a conscious effort on the part of the Congress to empower state and local party committees in federal campaigns. Soft money was first raised and spent in the 1980 elections, and it has grown from about $19 million in 1980 to $45 million in 1988, as shown in Table 3.3.

The Center for Responsive Politics made an independent study of soft money contributions to Democratic and Republican party committees in nine states in 1988 and found $28.5 million in such contributions made by individuals, businesses, labor unions, trade associations, and the Democratic and Republican National Committees. Contributions to the Republican state parties amounted to $16.7 million and to the Democrats, $11.8 million.[2] However, when the national party donations—$7.5 million to Democratic state committees and $2 million to Republican state committees—are subtracted, the amount reduces to $18.9 million. Analysis requires this calculation because the national party money was already accounted for in the $45 million total this book reports as raised and spent by Democrats and Republicans at the national level. Hence, the $45 million and the $28.5 million are not aggregative. Moreover, the $28.5 million figure includes contributions made throughout 1987 and early 1988, when presidential general election soft money spending was not even planned, with the exception of registration drives. As noted in Chapter 3, it was not until mid-1988 that national-level efforts were made to raise soft money for the presidential contests. In conclusion, the center's study overstates the amount of soft money but is useful in terms of its supplementary documentation in these nine states.

Of course, soft money also is raised and spent in senatorial and congressional campaigns, in lesser amounts; the documentation for this is in another Center for Responsive Politics publication.[3]

Soft Money and Team 100

Common Cause, among other reformers, has been highly critical of the concept of soft money in general and its use in the 1988 elections in particular. In the March/April 1990 issue of *Common Cause Magazine,* the cover story was the "Mosbacher Connection," an article that detailed the way the Bush campaign raised its soft money.[4] Although it did not include information on the manner in which the Dukakis campaign raised such funds, the article was valuable for the light it shed on soft money in the 1988 elections.

Robert Mosbacher did the same thing for George Bush that his opposite number, Robert Farmer, did for Michael Dukakis; as the chief fund-raisers, each took on the job of obtaining more than $20 million in soft money. Among their sources were corporations and labor unions, which are not allowed to contribute to federal candidates but may give funds at the state level in many cases. The fact that Mosbacher's and Farmer's solicitees consisted of donors giving well beyond federal limits, allowing for spending beyond the limits imposed on presidential campaigns, seems to have violated the spirit of the campaign finance limitations of 1974.

A California Case Study

One of the coauthors of this volume was able to obtain internal campaign records of the Democratic soft money operation for the Dukakis campaign in California in 1988. As a case study, the data give insight into the controversial subject of soft money.

Anthony Podesta was the Dukakis operative in California, and he ran both the hard and soft money aspects of Campaign '88, combining Campaign '88 and the California Democratic Party. Obviously, California was a major money state, with more than $5 million spent and hundreds of workers. Podesta even produced some spot announcements (using hard money) for California broadcasting, distinctive from those of the national Dukakis campaign.

California stretches from the north coast to the Mexican border and has 29,000 precincts. In early fall, Campaign '88 had 92 offices, more than 1 for each of the 80 assembly districts. In September, there were 175 paid workers, and the number expanded to 500 by election day. The campaign also claimed to have some 25,000 volunteers.[5] Money, both hard and soft, was solicited via a number of well-known fund-raisers and events, mainly in Los Angeles, San Francisco, and San Diego. Dukakis attended such events, where $1.5 million was claimed to have been raised. On one printout, Walter Shorenstein, a San Francisco entrepreneur, was credited with giving or raising $578,000. The Hollywood Women's Political Committee provided $230,000. Lieutenant Governor Leo McCarthy raised $55,000. And the Democratic National Committee provided about $3 million.

A Campaign '88 printout provided total expenditures as well as a breakdown of week-by-week spending over the last six weeks of the campaign. Totals for major expenditure categories are shown in Table 5.1.

TABLE 5.1
California Campaign '88, Hard and Soft Moneys Combined

Expenditures	Total
Headquarters operations	$ 753,638
Media	1,170,288
Polling	325,769
Absentee ballot	131,467
Voter registration	200,000
Political operations	124,271
Field staff	1,158,492
Field operations	1,217,741
Fund-raising	71,796
Extra budget operations	190,426
Total	$5,343,887

Source: Citizens' Research Foundation.

The Dukakis campaign spent about $1.2 million on its media, mainly television broadcasting of spot announcements, apart from the national advertising campaign that reached California. In contrast, Bush ads totaling at least $700,000 in Los Angeles and $400,000 in San Francisco were tracked.[6] Further breakdowns show some interesting selected expenditures subsumed under the major categories in Table 5.1, as follows:

Phones	$112,700
Postage	34,756
Polling	325,769
Autos	14,747
Voter registration	200,000
Absentee ballots	131,467
Surrogate travel	13,591
Buttons/stickers	51,799
Signs	166,121
Precinct maps	2,179
Sound trucks	6,000
FAX	3,286

Total expenditures were $3.5 million in soft money and $1.7 million in hard money, indicating an allocation of about 66–70 percent soft money. The spending was handled by individual bills being paid in either hard or soft dollars, with the overall mix at the allocation percentages. Legal and accounting costs, which are exempt from any hard money expenditure limits, amounted to $26,844.

From January 2 to September 9, the Democrats registered 479,685 voters, and the Republicans added 303,432. One of the direct mail drives went to 530,000 registered Democrats who did not vote regularly, part of an absentee ballot campaign.

Presidential voter turnout in California in 1988 was 47.4 percent, down 2.2 percent from 1984. George Bush received 51.1 percent of the vote, and Michael Dukakis got 47.6 percent, a higher percentage than recent Democratic presidential candidates had received.[7]

SOFT MONEY AND THE KEATING FIVE

The savings and loan debacle is the most expensive regulatory scandal in American history, with potential costs to taxpayers estimated in the hundreds of billions of dollars. The case of one savings and loan institution, Lincoln, received special attention as a result of $1.3 million in contributions made by its president, Charles H. Keating, Jr., and his family and associates. The contributions consisted of both hard and soft money, and they demonstrate a reality about political finance despite strict election laws.

Lincoln Savings and Loan was receiving close scrutiny in 1988 by federal regulators. Under pressure to close Lincoln, Keating and others made numerous political contributions; of special interest are those made to five U.S. senators or to soft money recipients they designated.

Keating made or arranged direct Senate contributions of $34,000 to John Glenn, $47,000 to Alan Cranston, $112,000 to John McCain, $55,000 to Dennis DeConcini, and $76,000 to Donald Riegle. In addition to the necessary bundling to reach these "hard money" contribution totals, Keating arranged $200,000 in soft money contributions to a committee operated by John Glenn—the National Council on Public Policy. He also arranged $850,000 in soft money contributions to committees working on voter registration and turnout in California; one of these tax-exempt committees was operated by Cranston's son. Cranston's fund-raising was in keeping with a long-standing commitment on his part to support such party-building activities; he had also introduced bills in the Senate to enhance voter registration and had raised considerable money for such purposes. Keating also gave $85,000 to the California Democratic State Central Committee for voter activities.[8] Further, it has been determined that American Continental Corporation, another company that Keating headed, gave $90,000 to the California Republican party in 1988 and that Lincoln Savings and Loan had given $5,000 to the California Republicans back in 1987.

The five senators involved, four Democrats and one Republican, were dubbed the "Keating Five" and were accused of having engaged in an extraordinary effort to help Keating. Initially, four of them—and in a second meeting, all five—summoned the chairman of the Federal Home

Loan Bank Board and key officials to discuss proposed actions against Lincoln, including the possibility of delays in the board's moving in on the institution.

When the relationships of Keating to the five senators became public, the senators all denied doing favors for him because of his political donations. Senators DeConcini, McCain, and Cranston claimed they were simply performing constituency service because Keating's holdings were mainly in Arizona, where he lived, and in California. Subsequently, Keating himself said in a news conference: "One question, among many, has had to do with whether my financial support in any way influenced several political figures to take up my cause. I want to say in the most forceful way I can: I certainly hope so."[9]

Although neither George Bush nor Michael Dukakis made an issue of the savings and loan crisis in the 1988 presidential campaigns, it was later revealed by Common Cause that the Bush-Republican party campaign received eight $100,000 soft money contributions from individuals related to various savings and loans. The same study listed the senators who received the most hard money contributions from savings and loans, both through individuals and PACs, in the 1980s.[10] They are:

Senator Pete Wilson (R–CA)	$243,334
Senator Donald Reigle (D–MI)	200,000
Senator Lloyd Bentsen (D–TX)	154,207
Senator Alan Cranston (D–CA)	143,700
Senator Alfonse D'Amato (R–NY)	88,235

The top recipients in the House in the 1980s include:

Representative William Lowery (R–CA)	$85,088
Representative David Dreier (R–CA)	75,150
Representative Mel Levine (D–CA)	69,250
Representative Richard Lehman (D–CA)	68,090
Representative Norman Shumway (R–CA)	67,425

It is interesting to note that two of the five senators and all five of the representatives are from California, a large savings and loan institution state.

In continuing developments, the Senate Ethics Committee appointed a special counsel, Robert S. Bennett, to investigate alleged ethics violations by the five senators. In July 1990, Senator Reigle, chairman of the Senate Committee on Banking, Housing, and Urban Affairs, announced he would donate about $120,000 of his savings and loan contributions to the federal treasury. Another senator, Tim Wirth (D–

CO), who was also on the Senate Banking Committee with Riegle, sent $98,950 to the Colorado Department of Revenue. Three other senators returned smaller amounts.[11]

In September 1990, Charles Keating and three of his associates were indicted for allegedly violating California securities laws by misleading investors about the nature of Lincoln bonds that were later termed "junk bonds." There were forty-two separate counts, and Keating was jailed when he failed to make a $5 million bond, later reduced to $300,000.[12] His earlier contributions (through his companies, business associates, and family) of $153,000 to a campaign committee of the Republican governor of California, George Deukmejian, and his assistance to the California Republican party did not deter the state from proceeding with the indictment.[13]

Despite contribution limits in federal law, large amounts in the aggregate can emanate from a single source or a related few sources, through soft money gifts and bundling of some $342,000. Obviously, the line between constituency service and undue influence is a thin one. Though some members of Congress said returning contributions was an admission of influence, others suggested the events would give impetus to efforts to achieve election reform in ways that would diminish "special interest" contributions.[14]

REGULATING SOFT MONEY

There have been sporadic attempts to regulate soft money. As early as 1984, Common Cause advocated rulemaking by the Federal Election Commission, but in 1986, the FEC denied the petition for rulemaking on the grounds that it lacked hard evidence. Common Cause sought relief in the courts, and the FEC was mandated to reconsider. In 1988, the FEC considered proposed rules but failed to promulgate them. The Congress was urged to act, but it did not do so.[15] Meanwhile, consensus seemed to grow to at least require disclosure of soft money.

Such disclosures had been made earlier, dating back to the 1980[16] and 1984[17] presidential campaigns and including a $1 million gift to the Democratic National Committee from Joan B. Kroc, then owner of the San Diego Padres and widow of the founder of the McDonald's restaurant chain.[18] Starting in 1988, the Democratic National Committee and then the Republican National Committee began to disclose voluntarily the sources of their state-related soft money, as well as some of the expenditures and transfers of funds to state organizations for soft money purposes.[19]

After fits and starts, years of deliberation, and some judicial prodding, the FEC moved. On June 21, 1990, it announced new regulations pertaining to soft money and sent them to the Congress for review as required by law.[20] They were promulgated in September 1990 and went into effect on January 1, 1991.

The new rules and allocation formulas, which relate to the disclosure of soft money, are complex. They apply to the national, senatorial, and congressional party committees, as well as to state and local party committees. During a presidential election year, the national parties must allocate at least 65 percent of the costs of generic voter drives and administrative expenses to their hard money accounts; the allocation is 60 percent in nonpresidential election years. Using a two-year election cycle for Senate and House campaigns, the allocation must be the greater of 65 percent or a ratio based on actual money spent for federal and nonfederal candidates.

Communication and phone bank costs are allocated differently, based on the relative benefit that each candidate receives from space in a publication or time on the air. Fund-raising costs are allocated according to the relative amounts of federal and nonfederal moneys raised. Further, state and local party committees must allocate generic voter drives and administrative costs based on the number of federal and nonfederal candidates on the ticket. And the identities of contributors who give to either soft money or building fund accounts in amounts of more than $200 must be disclosed.[21]

INDEPENDENT EXPENDITURES IN 1988

In its 1976 *Buckley* decision, the Supreme Court ruled that individuals and groups may spend unlimited amounts on communications advocating the election or defeat of clearly identified candidates, provided the expenditures are made without consultation or collaboration with the candidates or their campaigns.[22] Following the rulings, the 1976 FECA amendments imposed no limitations on independent expenditures on behalf of or in opposition to federal candidates. Individual donations to independent committees, however, are restricted to a maximum of $5,000 to each multicandidate committee and $1,000 to each single-candidate committee. Moreover, any contributions to committees making independent expenditures are counted against the contributor's $25,000 overall limit to all federal campaigns annually.

By 1980, groups and individuals inclined to make independent expenditures had developed sufficient familiarity with the election law to spend about $2.7 million in the presidential prenomination campaign, about $1.6 million of it reported as expenditures on Ronald Reagan's behalf. Subsequently, independent expenditures became the object of considerable litigation.

In July 1980, both Common Cause and the FEC filed suit against a number of groups that had announced plans to spend money independently on behalf of Reagan in the general election. Among other things, the complainants argued that the proposed independent spending would violate a provision of the Presidential Election Campaign Fund Act that prohibited organized political committees from spending more than $1,000 on behalf of a candidate eligible to receive public funds. The specific provision, Section 9012(f)(1) of the Internal Revenue Service Code, never was directly considered by the Supreme Court in *Buckley* and was left untouched when Congress rewrote the election law to conform with the court's ruling. A three-judge federal district court panel rejected the suits, striking down that section of the code as an unconstitutional restriction of the First Amendment rights of individuals. The complainants appealed the decision, but it was too late to affect independent spending in the 1980 general election. Groups and individuals reported spending substantial sums independently, with the bulk of it—$10.6 million—reported on Ronald Reagan's behalf. In January 1982, the U.S. Supreme Court upheld the fall 1980 appeals court decision by reaching a 4 to 4 deadlock in the case. Because the vote was equally divided, the Court's decision had no value as a precedent and applied only in the District of Columbia circuit.

Faced with the possibility that groups and individuals might spend large amounts independently on behalf of Reagan in the 1984 presidential campaign, the FEC and the Democratic National Committee brought suit in 1983 in the U.S. District Court for the Eastern District of Pennsylvania against the National Conservative Political Action Committee (NCPAC) and the Fund for a Conservative Majority (FCM), two groups that had announced plans to conduct pro-Reagan independent expenditure campaigns in 1984. The Pennsylvania district court refused to allow the FEC to implement Section 9012(f)(1), and the commission filed an appeal with the Supreme Court. The high court declined to expedite the appeal and did not hear oral arguments in the case until late November 1984, after the general election. In March 1985, the Court, in a 7 to 2 vote, struck down Section 9012(f)(1) of the IRS Code as unconstitutional.[23] Justice William Rehnquist, writing for the majority, declared that the provision failed to serve a compelling government interest, such as avoiding corruption or the appearance of it, and that, accordingly, the provision's restrictions of First Amendment rights could not be upheld. In dissent, Justice Byron White took issue with the Court's identification of money and speech, arguing, as he had in *Buckley,* that the First Amendment protects the right to speak, not the right to spend.

Some observers argue that in many cases in which the commission appears to be at odds with the First Amendment, the fault lies with the campaign law and not with the agency mandated to administer and defend it. That argument was made regarding the NCPAC case. Commission defenders maintain the FEC had no choice but to seek an injunction of NCPAC's proposed independent spending because Section 9012(f) of the Presidential Election Campaign Fund Act prohibited such spending beyond $1,000. In the light of a number of court decisions castigating the commission for its insensitivity to First Amendment rights, however, critics question whether involvement in such cases represents a wise use of FEC resources or an appreciation by the agency of the importance of freedom of speech in the political arena.

In the 1987–1988 election cycle, total independent expenditures decreased for the first time since such campaigns began. Total spending was pegged at $21.4 million, as shown in Tables 5.2 and 5.3, down from $23.4 million in 1983–1984.

INDEPENDENT EXPENDITURES AND CONGRESSIONAL ELECTIONS

Independent expenditure campaigns in congressional races tend to mirror the giving of other PACs: a heavy emphasis on supporting incumbents. One reason a PAC may lean toward independent expenditures is to get the attention and appreciation of the incumbent. This is especially true for trade and industry PACs, as opposed to ideological ones. An example cited by Candice J. Nelson is the growing independent expenditures of the Realtor's PAC.

> In 1984 the Realtors spent $355,000 in independent expenditures; in 1986 they spent $1.6 million, second only to the National Committee to Preserve Social Security. [In 1988, they were number one, contributing $3,045,769 to federal candidates.] Given the number of business PACs active in elections in the late 1980s, the Realtors felt that direct contributions to candidates no longer had the impact that they had a decade ago. "Not only has the PAC explosion devalued the political currency, but the value of campaign money has also been eroded by inflation. In that kind of environment, you're only deluding yourself if you think giving $5,000 to a candidate will have an impact on a campaign," said NAR [National Association of Realtors] vice president Gary South. The Realtors saw independent expenditures as an alternative to direct contributions, and an alternative with a potentially more direct impact on elections.[24]

TABLE 5.2
Independent Expenditures: Presidential and Vice Presidential, Prenomination and
General Election, 1988

	For	*Against*
General election		
Bush	$ 6,756,115	$ 77,325
Dukakis	567,623	2,671,728
Quayle	0	63,103
Bentsen	6,623	0
Subtotal	$ 7,330,361	$2,812,156
General election total	$10,142,517	
Prenomination[a]		
Bush	$ 3,004,532	$ 9,443
Dole	298,830	1,781
Dukakis	36,434	395,974
du Pont	814	3,720
Gephardt	15,170	22,681
Gore	3,070	12,252
Haig	0	817
Hart	0	35,353
Jackson	8,493	163,755
Kemp	30,567	1,781
Robertson	106,580	0
Simon	18,514	8,622
Subtotal	$ 3,523,004	$ 656,179
Prenomination total	4,179,183	
Total presidential	14,321,170	

[a]Presidential prenomination period includes all expenditures made through July
15 for the Democratic candidates and all expenditures made through August 15
for the Republicans.

Source: Federal Election Commission, 1987–1988. Candidate Index of Independent
Expenditures, as of August 20, 1990.

There was more independent money spent in favor of Republican
candidates: $13.7 million, compared with only $2.8 million for all
Democrats. The mirror image of this is seen in the spending against
a candidate, which showed $4.2 million in negative spending targeting
Democrats and $439,000 spent against Republicans. Despite lower overall
amounts in 1988, negative spending reached its highest level since
1982, when such spending totaled $5.1 million. In 1988, the negative
spending was $4.6 million.

TABLE 5.3
Congressional Elections and Independent Expenditures

	For	Against
Senate candidates	$3,641,161	$ 766,711
House candidates	2,271,691	446,487
Total congressional independent spending	$7,126,050	

Source: Federal Election Commission, 1987–1988. Candidate Index of Independent Expenditures, as of August 20, 1990.

Independent spending, though an important factor in political finance, should not be overrated. It has been noted that in every cycle of the 1980s, "the amount drops off precipitously" as one looks at the ten biggest spenders in this category. For example, the largest independent expenditure in 1988 was $8.3 million, spent by the National Security PAC; the tenth largest independent expenditure PAC, the Conservative Victory Committee, spent $318,877.[25] However, independent expenditures could grow if reform legislation outlawed PAC giving in its present form.

THE INDEPENDENT CAMPAIGN AND THE PRESIDENTIAL ELECTIONS

A group of Californians created an independent expenditure campaign to help George Bush, and their television spot, featuring a felon named Willie Horton, became the most controversial element of the 1988 campaigns for many journalists. This group, the Committee for the Presidency, spent only $92,000 to attack Michael Dukakis's record on crime. Such a sum ordinarily would not matter in a multi-million-dollar presidential campaign. But this commercial, with its image of a young black rapist and a voice-over detailing the prison program in Massachusetts that led to his furlough, escape, and the brutal rape of a Maryland woman, were so explosive they attracted the attention of the national press.

As part of the group's strategy, political consultant Lee Spitzberger put together a series of press conferences in California, Texas, New York, and Chicago, where Cliff Barnes, the fiancé of the woman raped in Maryland, discussed what Horton's escape from the Dukakis prison furlough program had done to his girlfriend. In the flurry of press coverage that ensued, members of the Committee for the Presidency saw its commercial aired on ABC's "Nightline" program and numerous evening newscasts, thus amplifying the effect of their original spending beyond their modest hopes. The ripple effect moved the Willie Horton episode into a major issue of the campaign, at no cost to the Bush camp.

Another independent group, the National Security Political Action Committee, ran its own Willie Horton advertisement on national cable television in September 1988. The PAC stopped running the Horton ads after receiving a letter from James Baker, chairman of the Bush campaign, asking it to cease. Even the national media, confused about the nature of independent campaigns, continued to refer to the Horton ad as a product of the Bush campaign, which it was not.

CAVEATS IN ANALYZING INDEPENDENT EXPENDITURES

One of the major problems in analyzing the influence of independently raised and spent moneys is deciding how much of what was spent could be labeled an activity in behalf of, or against, a candidate.

Title 11 of the Code of Federal Regulations of the FEC states that independent expenditures are "an expenditure for a communication expressly advocating the election or defeat of a clearly identified candidate that is not made with the cooperation or prior consent of, or in consultation with, or at the request or suggestion of any candidate or his/her authorized committees or agents." Thus, if a group mails a letter asking for funds to defeat candidate x or help candidate y, even though 100 percent of the moneys raised will pay for the mailing and nothing further is done to help or hurt x or y, that fund-raising letter is considered to be an expenditure in behalf of, or against, candidate x or y. If a number of candidates are mentioned, a formula is used to apportion parts of the mailing costs as independent expenditures in behalf of each candidate. For example, if a mailing has a senator's name in it, as well as a candidate for the presidency, the expenditure will be regarded as being partly spent in behalf of the Senate candidate. Whether these expenditures are of the same quality as funds spent directly on television, radio, or print ads in behalf of a senator, both are considered independent expenditures under current law, and the FEC reports them as such.

Some experts on political finance, such as Margaret Latus Nugent, question whether the spending figures of such groups accurately portray their effects on American politics. Nugent has been quoted as saying, "Of the $10 million spent by NCPAC on behalf of President Reagan in 1984, less than 10 percent was spent on media advertising, polling, and other standard campaign activities, compared to 85 percent spent on direct mail services and printing."[26]

According to a report in *Common Cause Magazine,* one of the largest independent expenditure groups was American Citizens for Political Action (ACPA). In the 1988 elections, "just 26 percent of ACPA contributions [went] directly to congressional or presidential candidates."[27] It is not unusual for a group raising money through direct mail to spend time "prospecting" for donors without raising much money, but groups such as ACPA seem not to move beyond that "prospecting" stage to substantial campaign spending.

ACPA showed the third largest increase in receipts among PACs from the 1986 to the 1988 cycle. This PAC raised $3,879,682 in 1988, double the amount raised in 1986, and spent $3,870,920. This made ACPA the ninth largest spending PAC of the cycle; 34.6 percent of that was used on independent expenditure campaigns. However, ACPA is able to call any fund-raising literature that mentions federal candidates part of the independent campaign, even if such letters are mailed only to those persons who already are supportive of, or against, that candidate. Bob Dolan, the head of ACPA, mailed from the Young Americans for Freedom lists, under the 1988 names "Reagan Political Victory Fund" and "Americans for Dole." The *Common Cause* report claims that the so-called "independent expenditures" of Dolan's enterprises were really "the costs of some of its fund-raising efforts."[28]

SHADOW PACs AND THE DIRECT MAIL INDUSTRY

Another investigative report on this issue isolated three PACs, including ACPA, because their letters looked so strikingly similar. In so doing, reporters uncovered a direct mail firm that was writing, printing, and mailing all three: Responsive Dynamics, Inc. (RDI). Along with ACPA, the other PACs were the Conservative Victory Committee (raising funds on behalf of an independent campaign for Jack Kemp) and the National Security Political Action Committee, ostensibly raising funds to help George Bush. So money sent to a committee to help Bush would end up in the hands of the parent direct mail company, which could use those funds to create direct mail pleas in behalf of its other clients: independent expenditure campaigns for Kemp and Dole. In 1988, ACPA spent 47.2 percent of its budget on Response Dynamics and its related companies, and the NSPAC spent 98.2 percent of its budget on RDI and its wholly owned subsidiary companies.[29] The Conservative Victory Committee, which raised the smallest amount of the three, gave 30 percent of its budget to RDI and related companies.[30]

The NSPAC spent more on independent expenditures than any other PAC in 1988: $8,552,666. George Bush filed a complaint against the

NSPAC, alleging "fraud, manipulative practices, and intentionally disregarding the FEC's reporting obligations."[31]

There is some question about whether a number of these independent expenditure groups are really "shadow PACs," created by direct mail marketers to become their customers. RDI has been accused by a former president of "growing their own clients" by asking friends to set up organizations that would exist solely to use the services of RDI. The difference between a real PAC that exists to help candidates and a "shadow PAC" that exists to make money for the direct mail industry calls for further research and perhaps legislation. It certainly adds confusion to any attempt to analyze the impact of indirect expenditure campaigns within the complex funding mechanisms of American politics.

NOTES

1. For a full study of soft money and the 1984 elections, see Herbert E. Alexander, *"Soft Money" and Campaign Financing* (Washington, D.C.: Public Affairs Council, 1986).

2. "Soft Money '88: Money and Politics," Center for Responsive Politics, Washington, D.C., 1989, pp. 5–46. The nine states are California, Colorado, Florida, Illinois, Missouri, North Carolina, Pennsylvania, Texas, and Washington.

3. "Soft Money—A Loophole for the '80s," Center for Responsive Politics, Washington, D.C., 1985, pp. 1–27.

4. Jean Cobb, Jeff Denny, Vicki Kemper, and Viveca Novak, "All the President's Donors," *Common Cause Magazine,* vol. 16, no. 2, March/April 1990, pp. 21–27, 38–39.

5. Keith Love, "Dukakis' California Hopes Rest on Turnout Drive," *Los Angeles Times,* October 30, 1988.

6. Karen Tumulty, "Hard-Hitting Dukakis Ads Set for California," *Los Angeles Times,* November 6, 1988; and Keith Love, "Bush Ads Stress Experience, Call for 'Gentler' U.S.," *Los Angeles Times,* September 7, 1988.

7. "Official 1988 Presidential Election Results," *Congressional Quarterly Weekly Report,* vol. 47, no. 3, January 21, 1989, p. 139.

8. "Contributions from Keating: Five Who Benefitted," *New York Times,* November 5, 1989.

9. Jack W. Germond and Jules Witcover, "Looking for a Smoking Gun on Campaign Funds," *National Journal,* vol. 21, no. 48, December 2, 1989, p. 2956.

10. "It's a Wonderful Life: S & L Investments on Capitol Hill," Common Cause study, Washington, D.C., June 1990, pp. 1–5.

11. "More Senators Empty S & L Donations from Campaign Accounts," *PACs & Lobbies,* August 15, 1990, p. 2.

12. Richard W. Stevenson, "Keating Indicted in Savings Fraud and Goes to Jail," *New York Times,* September 19, 1990.

13. Richard C. Paddock and Paul Jacobs, "Deukmejian Defends Samuelian," *Los Angeles Times,* December 2, 1989.

14. Chuck Alston, "Returning S & L Cash Raises Questions," *Congressional Quarterly,* vol. 48, no. 31, August 4, 1990, p. 2476.

15. Richard Sybert and Anthony Oncidi, "Soft Money Payments Constitute a Major Source of Unregulated, Indirect Campaign Finance for both Parties," *Los Angeles Lawyer,* June 1989, pp. 51–59.

16. Elizabeth Drew, *Politics and Money: The New Road to Corruption* (New York: Collier Books, Macmillan Publishing Company, 1983); and Herbert E. Alexander, *Financing the 1980 Election* (Lexington, Mass.: Lexington Books, 1983), pp. 367–440.

17. Ed Zuckerman, " 'Soft Money': A New Life for 'Fatcats'," *PACs & Lobbies,* January 16, 1985, p. 106, and "More DNC 'Soft Money' Accounts Found," *PACs & Lobbies,* February 6, 1985, pp. 1–3; also, Herbert E. Alexander and Brian A. Haggerty, *Financing the 1984 Election* (Lexington, Mass.: Lexington Books, 1987), pp. 329–342.

18. Paul Houston, "Kroc Presents $1 Million Gift to Democrats," *Los Angeles Times,* August 14, 1987.

19. Democratic National Committee, "Report of Non-Federal Receipts and Disbursements," August 15, 1988, pp. unnumbered; an identical title dated November 15, 1988; and Center for Responsive Politics, "1987–88 Soft Money Contributions to Nine State Parties," Washington, D.C., undated. Republican National Committee disclosures were not distributed, but reporters were permitted to view records, such as "GOP Releases Partial List of Soft-Money Contributors," *Campaign Practices Reports,* vol. 15, no. 19, October 3, 1988, p. 9.

20. Federal Election Commission, "Methods of Allocation Between Federal and Non-Federal Accounts; Payments, Reporting; Final Rule; Transmittal of Regulations to Congress," *Federal Register,* vol. 55, no. 123, July 26, 1990, pp. 26058–26073.

21. James A. Barnes, "New 'Soft' Money Rules," *National Journal,* vol. 22, no. 26, June 30, 1990, p. 1614.

22. 424 U.S. at 51.

23. *Federal Election Commission* v. *National Conservative Political Action Committee, et al.,* 105 S. Ct. 1459, 1985.

24. Candice J. Nelson, "Loose Cannons: Independent Expenditures," in Margaret Latus Nugent and John R. Johannes, *Money, Elections, and Democracy: Reforming Congressional Campaign Finance* (Boulder, Colo.: Westview Press, 1990), p. 59.

25. Ibid., p. 51.

26. Quoted in Nicholas C. McBride, "Candidates Aren't Only Ones Spending Big Political Bucks," *Christian Science Monitor,* April 20, 1988.

27. Vicki Kemper, "Send Money!" *Common Cause Magazine,* vol. 16, no. 3, May/June 1990, p. 31.

28. Ibid.

29. "Wronging the Right: Those Amazing PACmen and Their Incredible Money Machine," *Who's Mailing What: The Monthly Newsletter and Record of the Direct Marketing Archive,* July/August 1988, p. 20.

30. Ibid.

31. Keven Ann Willey, "Bush Camp Accuses Conservative PAC of Bid to Mislead," *The Arizona Republic,* September 24, 1988.

§ 6
COMMUNICATING WITH THE VOTERS

This chapter sets forth the laws and regulations governing political broadcasting. It also covers actual broadcast costs, describes several related studies, and traces developments relating to presidential debates and forums.

BROADCAST MEDIA REGULATIONS

Basic federal law governing candidates' use of broadcast media to appeal to the electorate is embodied in the Federal Communications Act of 1934, which is administered by the Federal Communications Commission (FCC). Section 315 of the act regulates political broadcasting. It reads, "If any licensee shall permit any person who is a legally qualified candidate for any public office to use a broadcasting station," he shall afford equal opportunities to all other such candidates for that office in the use of such broadcasting station."[1] Only circumstances in which candidates themselves appear on broadcasts are covered by Section 315. Appearances by spokespersons for candidates generally are covered by another FCC rule, the "Zapple Doctrine."

The equal opportunities requirement of Section 315 is triggered when the identity of a candidate who appears on a broadcast can reasonably be presumed to be known by the audience and when the appearance is of sufficient magnitude to be considered an integral part of the broadcast. The appearance does not necessarily have to be related to or make mention of an individual's candidacy in order to be considered a "use" and thereby entitling a political opponent to an equal opportunity to appear.

The equal opportunities requirement is not absolute. In 1959, Congress amended the law, exempting candidate appearances in four news situations: newscasts; news interviews; news documentaries, provided the candidate's appearance is incidental to the subject matter of the documentary; and on-the-spot coverage of news events. In 1960, Section 315 was suspended as it applied to presidential and vice presidential nominees. This one-time suspension permitted John Kennedy and Richard Nixon to appear in a series of broadcast debates without broadcasters' being required to provide equal opportunities for minor party candidates. Similar attempts to suspend Section 315 to allow presidential debates in 1964, 1968, and 1972 failed. In 1975, however, the FCC, in response to a petition filed by the Aspen Institute Program on Communication and Society, ruled that broadcast political debates qualify as exempt, on-the-spot coverage of news events if they are sponsored by outside parties and are covered contemporaneously.[2] This administrative ruling permitted presidential debates sponsored by the League of Women Voters to be broadcast in 1976, 1980, and 1984.

In November 1983, the FCC relaxed its 1975 ruling regarding broadcast debate sponsorship. In response to a petition filed by Henry Geller, former Carter administration Commerce Department official, the National Association of Broadcasters (NAB), and the Radio and Television News Directors Association, the commission ruled that broadcasters may stage their own debates, inviting political candidates of their choice to participate, without violating Section 315 provided the broadcasters do not favor or disfavor any particular candidate.[3] The commission also lifted its 1975 restriction limiting rebroadcast of political debates to within twenty-four hours of the original event. FCC Chairman Mark S. Fowler maintained the ruling would "encourage increased political debate, especially at the smaller and local levels."[4] Broadcasters, predictably, hailed the decision. Edward O. Fritts, NAB president, said it would allow the broadcast industry to better serve the public interest, noting that "the public and our form of government [are] the obvious winners."[5] Gene Mater, then senior vice president of CBS News, said he thought broadcasters would do a far better job of staging political debates than "people not in the business, who [are] not journalists."[6]

The 1983 FEC ruling was not universally acclaimed. Andrew Schwartzman, director of the Media Access Project, agreed with FCC Chairman Fowler that the ruling would have its greatest effect at the state and local levels. He warned, however, that local broadcasters' judgments about which candidates to include in a debate might be influenced by the broadcasters' business or family relationships. The League of Women Voters, which sponsored presidential forums and debates during the prenomination and general election campaigns in 1976 and 1980 and had already launched similar plans for 1984, strongly objected to the decision. The League's president, Dorothy S. Ridings, observed that the ruling permitted broadcasters to make, as well as cover, the news and made voters "even more vulnerable to the influence of the TV networks on campaigns and elections."[7] She upheld the League's position that debates should be sponsored by independent outside organizations that are nonpartisan and nonprofit. "Our purpose is not to entertain, it is to inform," she said.[8]

The League appealed the FCC decision, but in March 1984, the U.S. Court of Appeals in Washington issued a brief, unsigned, and unanimous judgment affirming the commission's ruling. The court held that the group's decision was a "legitimate exercise of its discretion."[9]

The Federal Election Commission has no jurisdiction over the broadcasting of candidate debates. However, it has been required to reconcile provisions of the FECA that prohibit contributions and expenditures by corporations in connection with federal elections with the FCC decisions to permit news media corporations first to broadcast debates staged by others and more recently to broadcast debates they themselves stage.[10] In 1979, the FEC prescribed regulations to create a narrow exception to the ban on corporate expenditures in connection with federal elections, thereby permitting news media organizations and certain nonprofit corporations to sponsor nonpartisan candidate debates.[11] Under the exception, debate structure is left to the discretion of the staging organization, provided the debate includes at least two candidates and is nonpartisan—that is, that it does not promote or advance one candidate over another.[12] The FEC promulgated these regulations because it considered the staging of candidate debates to be outside an existing exemption from the law's definition of "expenditure" money spent by news media corporations on news stories, commentaries, or editorials.[13] The 1983 FCC decision, however, clearly included broadcaster sponsorship of candidate debates within a broadcast media organization's news function. Accordingly, the FEC was faced with the decision whether to revise its regulations to follow the FCC's 1983 interpretation or to retain the approach the FEC formulated in 1979. In large part because it wanted to avoid suggesting that all activities of broadcasters were to be exempted from the FECA requirements, the election commission chose to retain its 1979 regulations.

1988 DEBATES AND FORUMS

Although the 1984 debates, like those in 1976 and 1980, were sponsored by the League of Women Voters, developments led to political party sponsorship of the general election debates in 1988. A Commission on National Elections, sponsored by the Center for Strategic and International Studies, released a report in April 1986 that called for the institutionalization of joint appearances by major party nominees for the presidency.[14] It was proposed that, in order to improve voter education, the two political parties should assume direct responsibility for sponsoring the debates, subject to candidate acceptance. One reason for this was that in all prior presidential campaigns in which there were debates, protracted negotiations among candidates and sponsors often threatened to undermine the debates themselves.

Therefore, a Memorandum of Agreement on Presidential Candidate Joint Appearances, signed by Democratic National Committee Chairman Paul G. Kirk, Jr., and Republican National Committee Chairman Frank J. Fahrenkopf, Jr., was included in the report.[15] Subsequently, in early 1987, a bipartisan, nonprofit organization was established, called the Commission on Presidential Debates. On behalf of the parties, the commission conducted four general election debates—three between the presidential candidates and one between the vice presidential candidates. The funding for the commission and the debates was derived mainly from corporations and foundations.

Under other sponsorship, almost two dozen debates—better called forums—were scheduled in the prenomination period, but a few were canceled. Starting in October 1987 and running through April 1988, they were held in various locations, ranging from the Kennedy Center in Washington, D.C., to Des Moines, Iowa, to several locations in New Hampshire and others southward and westward. The appearances, some featuring as many as 7 candidates, were sponsored by groups including television programs, newspapers, state party committees, and the League of Women Voters.

REASONABLE ACCESS

Although Section 315 of the Communications Act of 1934 requires broadcast stations to afford political candidates equal opportunities to appear or to respond in the circumstances described, it does not require stations to allow candidates to appear in the first place. Another section of the act, Section 312(a)(7), however, warns licensees that among grounds for revocation of their licenses include the "willful or repeated failure to allow reasonable access to or to permit purchase of reasonable amounts of time for the use of a broadcasting station by a legally qualified candidate for federal elective office on behalf of his candidacy."[16] State and local candidates are not mentioned in this section, but the FCC interprets Section 307 of the act (which grants licenses only "if the public convenience, interest or necessity will be served thereby"[17]) to mean, among other things, that stations cannot choose to avoid equal opportunities requirements simply by refusing to provide political candidates with any access to their facilities. Even state and local candidates must be given access, although there is no fixed formula by which to measure reasonableness in that case.

Section 312(a)(7) does not require broadcast licensees to sell broadcast time to candidates at any level. Rather, licensees may fulfill the requirement this provision imposes by inviting candidates for specific offices to participate in forums and debates.[18] The requirement, stipulating that some broadcast time—whether purchased or free—must be made available, became a matter of litigation during the 1980 presidential campaigns. The three major commercial television networks refused to sell candidates Ronald Reagan, Jimmy Carter, and John Connally broadcast time late in 1979 to announce and promote their presidential candidacies, maintaining that it was much too early for such advertisements. When the FCC sided with the Carter campaign committee, which had filed a complaint based on the reasonable access provision of the law, the networks brought suit against the FCC. The matter was carried to the Supreme Court, which ruled in July 1981 that the First Amendment rights of candidates to present their views and of voters to obtain information outweigh the constitutional rights of broadcasters.

LOWEST UNIT RATE

If a broadcast licensee does sell time to a candidate, it must do so in accordance with a provision of the FECA, according to which Section 315(b) of the Communications Act was amended. Under this provision, the broadcast media cannot charge political candidates more than the lowest unit rate charged to any other advertiser for the same class and amount of time in the forty-five days before a primary election and sixty days before a general or special election. At other times, rates cannot exceed the charges made for comparable use for other purposes. Thus, during the designated campaign period, political candidates are to be given the same discounts as a broadcast station's most favored advertiser.

Some broadcasters, however, have succeeded in frustrating the lowest unit rate provision by making it available only on an immediately preemptible basis. "If a candidate does not like the idea that his announcement may be pre-empted," explained political consultant and media time buyer Jack Fiman at a 1983 congressional hearing, "he can elect to pay a fixed rate—usually the highest rate ever offered, but almost never used by regular clients of the stations. Television stations have interpreted the lowest unit rate to mean that they offer the lowest rate with no guarantee of airing and a choice of paying a higher rate in order to secure the desired time."[19] Thus, despite the lowest unit rate provision, candidates who feel strongly that their advertising must air at specific times in the weeks before an election often have no choice but to pay the high rates charged by the stations for fixed time.

A Federal Communications Commission audit of thirty television and radio stations in five selected cities during part of the 1990 election year produced preliminary findings that indicated they had been charging political candidates more money than other customers to broadcast advertisements. In one city in a week-long span, all candidates paid in excess of the highest rate paid by any commercial advertiser. In another case, candidates paid an average of $6,000 for a thirty-second spot announcement, although the average cost for commercial advertisers was $2,713. The FCC also found that some stations created new classes of time for candidates, called "news adjacencies," for which there were no comparable commercial rates; hence, higher charges were made.[20] One reason for these excessive charges is that most candidates seek to buy fixed air time, at a specific time aimed to reach certain audiences. Such time traditionally has drawn higher rates than preemptible air time, wherein there is no guarantee that a spot will be broadcast if other advertisers are willing to pay higher rates for the time. But if an election is imminent, candidates are often willing to pay higher rates for the time the consultants and media buyers tell them they need. Although the FCC audit was conducted in 1990, its findings would no doubt have been applicable at some stations in 1988 as well. Ultimately, they moved the FCC to rule that broadcasters must stop charging premium rates for political advertising on television and radio.

Since 1972, federal law has required broadcasters to sell political time at the lowest unit charge, giving candidates a price comparable to the lowest rate sold to a most favored advertiser for a spot in a comparable time period. Certain broadcasters auction off given time periods to the highest bidder, political or commercial. One can conclude that some stations have not been fair to political candidates and that some political consultants and time buyers have not bargained for the better rates required by law. Moreover, some observers maintain that high television costs are a cause of negative advertising because candidates cannot afford softer positive spots but must instead resort to hard-hitting negative spots to get their messages across.[21]

THE COSTS OF TELEVISION

Among the few functional expenditures that have been tabulated across the country at all levels, the most prominent is political advertising on television. The Television Bureau of Advertising estimated that $227,900,200 was spent on political television advertising and programs in 1988: $38,520,700 on networks and $189,379,500 on local spot announcements.[22] The remarkable finding is that this represents only 8.4 percent of total political spending. This small percentage tends to dispel the widely held notions that television is a large political expense, that television ads are pervasive, and that they have changed the face of American politics.

According to a calculation by the U.S. Census Bureau in 1987, there were 504,404 popularly elected offices in the United States.[23] A large portion of these officeholders were elected in the 1987–1988 election cycle, accounting for the candidate portion of the $2.7 billion total political spending reported in Chapter 1. But most of the candidates for these offices never buy any television advertising time nor even get near a television camera. Usually, only serious candidates for major offices—presidential, senatorial, and gubernatorial—make substantial use of television advertisements. Probably only about one-half of the House candidates purchase television time, and its cost often represents just a small portion of their campaign spending.

Even in races for some major offices (including the presidency) in which television advertising is essential, the extent of its use varies according to campaign strategy and circumstances. In the 1988 campaigns, the gross amounts spent on television air time (excluding production costs) by 5 major presidential candidates seeking nomination were $12.7 million of the $199.6 million all the candidates spent, or only 6 percent. In contrast, in the presidential general election campaigns, television expenditures were $52.5 million (57 percent) of the $92.2 million spent by the major party candidates' campaigns or 48 percent of the combined candidate and party-coordinated expenditures within the candidates' control, which amounts to $108.8 million.

The costs of television in a given election year are difficult to pinpoint due to the design of the FEC disclosure forms. For example, the costs of writing, producing, and running the spot may be hidden in other categories on the disclosure form—such as the unspecified "consultant" category—making it difficult to ascertain the exact broadcast-related costs. The Television Bureau of Advertising figures show the growing

TABLE 6.1
Costs of Political Advertising in Presidential Years, 1972–1988

	Network	Spot/Local	Total
1972	$ 6,519,100	$ 18,061,000	$ 24,580,100
1976	7,906,500	42,935,700	50,842,200
1980	20,699,700	69,870,300	90,570,000
1984	43,652,500	110,171,500	153,824,000
1988	38,520,700	189,379,500	227,900,200

Source: Joel L. Swerdlow, ed., *Media Technology and the Vote: Source Book,* The Annenberg-Washington Program (Boulder, Colo.: Westview Press, 1988), pp. 83–84. Figures for 1988 added.

costs of airing advertisements for political campaigns in aggregate terms, combining federal, state, and local candidates and committees. (See Table 6.1.)

As noted, not every candidate uses television advertising. For some, it is simply too expensive. Most House challengers, for example, did not raise enough money in 1988 to produce and run a single professionally written television spot. Then there are the cases of incumbents running without opposition who would appear foolish to voters if they spent a great deal of money on television advertisements. And House candidates whose districts are covered by the costliest media markets—such as New York City, which includes forty congressional districts in a tristate area—are more likely to spend their money on direct mail and radio rather than buy television time that blankets not only their district but sections of huge metropolitan areas whose viewers are unable to vote for the candidate. And there are many local campaigns for which television is simply not cost-efficient.

The differences between campaigns that cannot afford television, campaigns that find television less cost-effective than other means of communication, and campaigns where television is the central focus led to much confusion over a 1987 report on television spending by U.S. Senate and House candidates. The National Association of Broadcasters commissioned a study, done by Aristotle Industries using FEC reports, to rebut the charge that the growing costs of television were running behind the escalating costs of political campaigns generally. In a 1987 press release, the NAB stated that "candidates for federal office spent 24.3 percent of their budgets to buy television and radio time in 1986" and that "when Congress debates proposed reforms in campaign financing, it should have the facts."[24]

When the NAB chairman, Edward O. Fritts, released the study, he criticized a prevalent "let's go after TV attitude."[25] Congressman Al Swift (D–WA), chairman of the House Subcommittee on Elections and a former broadcaster, disagreed with the findings, noting that the data averaged open-seat, unopposed, and contested elections. He pointed out that by averaging the costs of the Zschau–Cranston Senate campaign in California with those of other Senate and House candidates who did not have serious opponents, the results were skewed.[26]

Although the NAB study showed that House candidates in 1988 spent just 15.8 percent of their budgets for total TV and radio time, with an additional 4 percent on production, and Senate candidates spent 33.7 percent on TV and radio time, with 5.2 percent on production, campaign professionals also were critical of the study. Frank Greer, a Washington consultant, said, "The report lumps together all races, without accounting for the contested races in marginal districts. . . . I guarantee you that in those cases, you're talking 75 or 80 percent of your budget on media."[27] Another consultant specializing in Senate races said that "politics is television today in a Senate race."[28]

Robert Squier, a prominent political consultant who generally works for candidates facing serious competition, says this about broadcast costs: "Our rule of thumb is that half the campaign money goes to paid media, and with our fee, it goes up to about 60 percent."[29] The discussion of television broadcast costs is further developed in the following section.

EXPENDITURES FOR CAMPAIGN SERVICES

The literature contains relatively few works categorizing campaign expenditures.[30] For selected congressional campaigns in 1988, the Congressional Research Service (CRS) undertook an innovative study focusing on various classifications of mainly communications expenditures in a sample of competitive Senate and House general election contests.[31] The findings were based on 18 Senate candidates and 63 House candidates who responded to the survey questionnaire; all ran in contests where the winner received less than 60 percent of the general election vote.

An overview of the CRS findings is given in Table 6.2 for the Senate and Table 6.3 for the House. The tables give insight into percentages of moneys spent in various categories, and the media classifications and polling data permit some generalizations:

- Combining costs for all media—television, radio, print, and production—Senate campaigns spent a median of 59.5 percent in this broad communications classification, whereas House campaigns spent 42.5 percent. Clearly, television advertising is dominant in

TABLE 6.2
Senate Expenditures for Campaign Services: 1988 General Election

Expenditure	Dollars	Percentage[a]
Television air time	$22,545,000	43.0
Television ad production	3,279,096	6.3
Radio air time	2,095,866	4.0
Radio ad production	484,380	.9
Print ad space	1,738,332	3.3
Print ad production	546,876	1.0
Postage	2,901,006	5.5
Other mail costs	3,108,780	5.9
Polls	2,220,966	4.2
Other services	13,492,314	25.7
	$52,412,616	99.8

[a]Weighted average, based on dollars spent.

Source: Joseph E. Cantor and Kevin J. Coleman, "Expenditures for Campaign Services: A Survey of 1988 Congressional Candidates in Competitive Elections," in "CRS Report for Congress," Congressional Research Service, Library of Congress, Washington, D.C., September 12, 1990, appendix B, pp. 91–126; addendum entitled "Summary Data on 1988 Congressional Candidates' Expenditure Survey," November 8, 1990, p. 5.

TABLE 6.3
House Expenditures for Campaign Services: 1988 General Election

Expenditure	Dollars	Percentage[a]
Television air time	$ 7,181,937	25.1
Television ad production	1,603,476	5.6
Radio air time	2,138,283	7.5
Radio ad production	397,341	1.4
Print ad space	583,317	2.0
Print ad production	267,624	.9
Postage	2,796,570	9.8
Other mail costs	3,149,874	11.0
Polls	1,699,803	5.9
Other services	8,792,532	30.7
	$28,610,757	99.9

[a]Weighted average, based on dollars spent.

Source: Joseph E. Cantor and Kevin J. Coleman, "Expenditures for Campaign Services: A Survey of 1988 Congressional Candidates in Competitive Elections," in "CRS Report for Congress," Congressional Research Service, Library of Congress, Washington, D.C., September 12, 1990, appendix A, pp. 55–90; addendum entitled "Summary Data on 1988 Congressional Candidates' Expenditure Survey," November 8, 1990, p. 3.

Senate campaigns, and radio and print are more popular in the House campaigns.

- There are striking differences in the portion of total campaign spending allocated to television air time: 43 percent for Senate campaigns and only 25.1 percent for House campaigns. Many House candidates do not buy television time because it is not cost-efficient to reach only a partial audience (in a single district) within an audience range that is much larger and therefore much more expensive than most campaigns can sustain.
- Production costs for television and radio ads run as high as 25 percent of air time costs.
- Understandably, radio is used relatively more by House campaigns than by Senate campaigns.
- Polling costs comprise similar percentages for Senate and House campaigns.
- Even in House campaigns, the professionalization of politics through the use of campaign consultants is apparent; for all media and polling services, professional campaign consultants must be widely employed.
- Other services include costs for salaries, headquarters, travel, registration and get-out-the-vote drives, research, and other expenses; expenses such as these are probably higher in the many House campaigns that do not use television (that is, those that are not in competitive districts and hence not covered in this study).

One can assume that if all Senate and House campaigns, competitive or not, were included, the use of television would remain high in the Senate campaigns even in noncompetitive contests, whereas in House campaigns, the percentage of television usage would decline and the percentage of other services would increase.

One additional finding in the CRS study is not presented in the tables. The candidates were asked to estimate the percentages of spending in primary and general election campaigns, even though only general election expenses were categorized. The totals follow:

	Mean	Median	Dollars
Senate			
Primary	30.0	35.0	$27,668,970
General election	70.3	65.0	52,412,616
House			
Primary	23.8	22.0	8,915,872
General election	76.1	78.0	28,611,009

Because the Federal Election Commission data on candidate spending do not distinguish between the primary and general election, these percentages are the only such data available.

To give some notion of the sample in dollar terms, the Senate portion of counted expenditures for the general election totaled $52.4 million, or 28 percent of the $185.3 million reported spent by all primary and general election candidates. The House portion of the general election costs were $28.6 million of the $222.3 million total spent by all, or 13 percent. More meaningful percentages could have been calculated had FEC reports distinguished between primary and general election spending.

The CRS survey is not directly comparable to the 1987 NAB report for the CRS used a questionnaire directed at candidates and the NAB used FEC reports. But the two, taken together, are important if they lead analysts to differentiate Senate and House campaigns in terms of political broadcast usage.

A LOS ANGELES SURVEY

Television costs in 1988 are illustrated in more detail by a local survey done by one of the coauthors of this volume, examining the broadcast logs of a Los Angeles television station—KNBC, Channel 4.

The Democratic National Committee was listed as sponsor of the following spots:

Date	Length	Cost	Time Slot	Time Aired
8/13	60 sec.	$ 2,200	SA, 4:58–6:30 P.M.	4:58 P.M.
8/13	60 sec.	30,000	SA, 8:58–10:00 P.M.	8:58 P.M.
8/14	60 sec.	24,000	SU, 8:58–11:00 P.M.	10:24 P.M.
8/15	60 sec.	1,900	MO, 6:68–8:58 A.M.	6:58 A.M.

Bush-Quayle '88 sponsored spot announcements as follows:

Date	Length	Cost	Time Slot	Time Aired
10/8	30 sec.	$15,000	SA, 8:58–10:00 P.M.	9:28 P.M.
10/11	30 sec.	2,000	TU, 6:58–8:58 P.M.	7:05 P.M.
10/11	30 sec.	4,700	TU, 11:01–11:30 P.M.	11:29 P.M.
10/13	30 sec.	725	TH, 2:58–3:58 P.M.	3:43 P.M.
10/18	30 sec.	1,300	TU, 6:58–8:58 P.M.	6:58 P.M.
10/18*	30 sec.	25,000	TU, 5:30–8:00 P.M.	9:00 P.M.
10/19*	30 sec.	25,000	WE, 5:30–8:00 P.M.	5:19 P.M.
10/26	30 sec.	9,000	WE, 8:58–10:00 P.M.	9:44 P.M.
10/28	30 sec.	2,900	FR, 6:28 P.M.	6:28 P.M.

*World Series

There was considerable variation in cost. From October 4 through November 7, the lowest price for thirty seconds of air time was $725; the highest, during the World Series, was $25,000. The greatest price paid for regularly scheduled air time was $15,000, during prime time on Saturday. From October 25–31, Bush-Quayle '88 spent $59,475 on commercial air time at KNBC; from November 1–7, Bush-Quayle '88 spent $75,575.

Air time for Dukakis-Bentsen Committee, Inc., was of course set at the same rates. Therefore, only those purchases that were substantially different from those of Bush-Quayle '88 are included below:

Date	Length	Cost	Time Slot	Time Aired
10/14	60 sec.	$14,000	FR, 9:00–10:00 P.M.	n/a
10/15	60 sec.	9,400	SA, 8:58 P.M.	n/a
10/27	30 sec.	18,000	TH, 9:58–11:00 P.M.	n/a
11/01	30 sec.	20,000	TU, 8:58–11:00 P.M.	n/a
11/03	30 sec.	27,000	TH, 9:28–11:00 P.M.	n/a

From October 25–31, Dukakis-Bentsen spent $61,275 on air time at KNBC; from November 1–7, $86,775.

The conclusion is that television purchases can be very expensive— all of these amounts were, after all, spent on just one Los Angeles station—but considering total political costs at all levels, the amounts spent on political broadcasting are minimal. Of course, if generalizations can be drawn from the 1990 FCC audit noted above—but without reference to the Los Angeles survey—political candidates may be charged excessive amounts by some stations.

Another report merits attention as well. A commission sponsored by the Markle Foundation reported that many Americans are "dangerously disconnected" from the political process. The Commission on the Media and the Electorate blames the behavior of candidates, the institutional setting in which they campaign, and the actions of the media. Money enables candidates and parties to persuade without really informing the electorate. The commission made a series of recommendations, several of which relate to the financing of campaigns. These call, among other things, for mandated debates with public funding conditioned on candidates' participation; for free public service air time during presidential campaigns; and for matching funds to be available only within the calendar year in which the election occurs.[32]

COMMUNICATION COSTS IN
THE 1988 PRESIDENTIAL CAMPAIGNS

In addition to the independent expenditure campaigns noted in Chapter 5, there is another form of participation by groups not affiliated with the candidate that falls outside the FEC guidelines on PACs. This is the so-called "communication costs" category of partisan political spending on restricted classes of persons, sanctioned by the Federal Election Campaign Act. Under the law, corporations, labor unions, and trade, membership, and health organizations may conduct four types of unlimited partisan communications: (1) meetings between candidates or political party representatives and the organizations' restricted classes; (2) printed publications written and produced by the organizations; (3) telephone banks; and (4) voter registration and turnout drives. The costs of partisan communications that aggregate more than $2,000 per election must be reported to the FEC by the organizations that conduct them, unless those communications are primarily devoted to subjects other than candidate advocacy. In that case, no reporting is required.

During the 1987–1988 election cycle, a total of almost $4.2 million was reported by various organizations as the costs of communications advocating the election of specified candidates; some $185,000 was listed as the costs of communications advocating the defeat of specified candidates. The reporting organizations spent almost $2 million of the total on communications advocating the election of specified presidential candidates and some $155,000 advocating the defeat of such candidates, as shown in Table 6.4. The remainder was spent on candidates for the House and Senate.

Communication costs decreased from 1984, when $4.7 million was spent in behalf of and some $48,000 was spent against a particular candidate in the presidential campaign. Spending in Senate and House campaigns in 1984, 1986, and 1988 was near $2 million in each case. Communication cost spending in 1988 Senate campaigns accounted for about $1.2 million in behalf of and $29,000 against given candidates; the House figures were about $1.1 million for and zero against.

No data are available regarding the amounts of money spent on partisan communications that did not reach the $2,000 reporting threshold or on communications advocating the election or defeat of candidates that were part of larger communications (such as regularly published newsletters) devoted primarily to subjects other than candidate advocacy. Nor is it possible to determine with precision the value of ostensibly nonpartisan communications, which in fact were targeted to reap maximum benefit for specific candidates or parties. Such communications

TABLE 6.4
Communication Costs: 1988 Presidential Campaigns

	Primary		General Election	
	For	Against	For	Against
George Bush	$ 450	none	$ 9,174	$104,404
Michael Dukakis	130,147	51,095	1,807,593	none
Lloyd Bentsen	none	none	13,289[a]	none
Jesse Jackson	28,295	none	none	none
Al Gore	812	none	none	none
Richard Gephardt	14	none	none	none
Subtotal	$159,718	$51,095	$1,830,850	$104,404
Total		$210,813		$1,934,460

[a]This figure represents funds specifically spent on Lloyd Bentsen's vice-presidential campaign; it does not include other funds spent on his Senate campaign.

Source: Federal Election Commission, 1987–1988. Communication Costs Index by Communication Filers, as of August 20, 1990.

include the publication of incumbents' voting records, voting guides describing candidates' positions, and joint sponsorship of nonpartisan voter drives with nonpartisan, tax-exempt organizations or state and local election administration agencies. Costs for these types of communications may be paid out of treasury funds, but the payments need not be reported to the FEC.

The membership groups most likely to incur "communication costs" are labor unions, which explains why so much was spent in support of Dukakis. Most of the largest labor unions give the maximum allowable contributions to their endorsed federal candidates through their PACs. And they are free to spend whatever they feel is needed to communicate with their members about their endorsement of a particular candidate. This is the equivalent of a direct mail campaign in behalf of a candidate but is nonetheless considered as a "communication cost," apart from other political spending.

In the 1984 prenomination period, organized labor had endorsed Walter Mondale in the Democratic primaries. Some local labor leaders felt a backlash from this for many of their rank and file supported other candidates, particularly Gary Hart. In 1988, the AFL-CIO decided not to endorse anyone in the primaries and caucuses, leaving individual unions free to endorse or fail to endorse any candidate. Most unions sat out the volatile prenomination season and waited until the general election to weigh in with their communications in behalf of a candidate.

Because most labor unions consider themselves part of the Democratic coalition, it is not surprising that very little was spent in favor of Republican candidates. However, it is notable that most of their communication costs were for positive endorsements, with very little spent on negative attacks.

NOTES

1. 47 U.S.C.A., Sect. 315.

2. Aspen Institute, 55 F.C.C. 2d 697 (1975), *aff'd sub nom. Chisolm* v. *F.C.C.,* 538 F.2d 349 (D.C. Cir. 1976).

3. Regarding petitions of Henry Geller and the National Association of Broadcasters and the Radio-Television News Directors Association to Change Commission Interpretation of Certain Subsections of the Communications Act, BC Docket 82-564, FCC 83-529 (released November 16, 1983), 48 Fed. Reg. 53166 (November 25, 1983).

4. Quoted in Penny Pagano, "FCC Broadens Rule on Equal Time for Debates," *Los Angeles Times,* November 9, 1983.

5. Quoted in Phil Gailey, "F.C.C. Lets Broadcasters Hold Political Debates," *New York Times,* November 9, 1983.

6. Quoted in Michael Isikoff, "Networks Win in '84 Debates," *Washington Post National Weekly Edition,* November 21, 1983.

7. Quoted in Gailey, op. cit.

8. Quoted in Isikoff, op. cit.

9. Quoted in Robert B. Abeshouse, "FCC Watch: On the Impact of Televised Debates and Advertising," *Campaigns & Elections,* vol. 5, no. 1, Spring 1984, p. 41.

10. 2 U.S.C. 441B.

11. See 11 CRF 110.13; also 110.7(b)(21), 100.8(b)(23), and 114.4(e).

12. For a discussion of the circumstances surrounding the 1979 candidate debate regulations, see Herbert E. Alexander and Brian A. Haggerty, *Financing the 1980 Election* (Lexington, Mass.: Lexington Books, 1983), pp. 155-158.

13. 2 U.S.C. 431(9)(B)(i).

14. Robert E. Hunter, ed., *Electing the President: A Program for Reform,* final report of the Commission on National Elections (Washington, D.C.: Center for Strategic and International Studies, 1986), pp. 41-44.

15. Ibid., back cover.

16. 47 U.S.C.A., Sect. 312(a)(7).

17. 47 U.S.C.A., Sect. 307.

18. Use of Broadcast and Cablecast Facilities, 37 Fed. Reg. 5796, 5805, Q and A 4, 5 (1972).

19. U.S., Congress, House, Committee on House Administration, Task Force on Elections, *Campaign Finance Reform,* 1984 Hearings, 98th Cong., 1st Sess. (Washington, D.C.: U.S. Government Printing Office, 1984), p. 684.

20. Federal Communications Commission, Washington, D.C., "Mass Media Bureau Report on Political Programming Audit," September 7, 1990, pp. 1-8.

21. Thomas B. Rosenthiel, " 'Candidates' Ad Rates Too High, FCC Says," *Los Angeles Times,* September 8, 1990.

22. "Political Advertising on Television," Television Bureau of Advertising, New York, press release, undated. The estimate for local spot announcements covers only the top 75 markets representing about 85 percent of projected political buys.

23. Richard Morin, "A Half a Million Choices for American Voters," *Washington Post National Weekly Edition,* February 6–12, 1989, p. 38.

24. "1986 Candidates Spent Less Than 25% of Funds on Broadcast Time; NAB Calls Focus of Campaign-Cost Debate on Radio, TV Unwarranted," National Association of Broadcasters, Washington, D.C., press release, July 13, 1987, pp. 1–2.

25. "NAB Lobbies Congress with First Ever Schedule B Database, Encounters Resistance on the Hill," *Campaign Industry News,* Washington, D.C., August 1987, p. 15.

26. Ibid.

27. Quoted in Andrew Rosenthal, "On the Air: $97 Million Spent in '86," *New York Times,* July 14, 1987.

28. Ibid.

29. Quoted in Dom Bonafede, "Costly Campaigns: Consultants Cash In as Candidates Spend What They Must," *National Journal,* April 16, 1983, p. 790.

30. See, for example, Edie N. Goldenberg and Michael W. Traugott, *Campaigning for Congress* (Washington, D.C.: CQ Press, 1984), pp. 77–92.

31. Joseph E. Cantor and Kevin J. Coleman, "Expenditures for Campaign Services: A Survey of 1988 Congressional Candidates in Competitive Elections," in "CRS Report for Congress," Congressional Research Service, Library of Congress, Washington, D.C., September 12, 1990; addendum entitled "Summary Data on 1988 Congressional Candidates' Expenditure Survey," November 8, 1990, pp. 1–5.

32. The Markle Commission on the Media and the Electorate, *Recommendations* (New York: The Markle Foundation, 1990), pp. 1–11.

7
EPILOGUE:
SHAPING ELECTION REFORM
HERBERT E. ALEXANDER

Following the 1988 congressional elections, House incumbents held 25 percent more cash in reserve than their challengers had spent in the entire campaign.[1] And the reelection rate in the House topped 98 percent for the second election cycle in a row.[2] Few would argue that these two sets of statistics were unrelated.

Because the instinct for self-preservation is strong in the political animal, it is not surprising that election law formulated by incumbents should also hold advantages for them. Public policy governing the financing of federal elections—enacted and fine-tuned in the 1970s—helped to establish a system that produced a steadily increasing incumbent share of campaign funds throughout the 1980s. PAC money made a corresponding surge, steadily expanding its availability while sharpening its focus on contributions to incumbents. Meanwhile, challenger candidacies declined in their ability to wage competitive monetary campaigns.

Despite the increased job security derived from contributions to incumbents, a movement to reform the campaign finance system took hold on Capitol Hill in the late 1980s and has been slowly edging toward enactment ever since. Although a few congressional Democrats have helped lead this movement (most notably Democratic Senator David Boren of Oklahoma), a great deal of prodding has come from the Republican party leadership and from public interest groups (principally Common Cause and Public Citizen). Each group sees a frightening specter on the horizon: for the "good government" lobby, an "Imperial Congress" or a "Permanent Congress" beholden to special interest money and oblivious to the public good; for the Republican chieftains, a frozen status quo locking them into what portends to be a perpetual minority status.

The pressure for reform became particularly acute in 1990, as the savings and loan scandal convinced many voters that special interest campaign contributions could wind up costing them thousands of dollars in additional taxes. The nearly successful effort by Congress to raise its own salaries by 50 percent the year before had left the voters with considerable suspicion that assured tenure would insulate representatives from the public will. A campaign to limit congressional careers to a twelve-year tour met with approval in polls and editorial pages across America.[3]

Yet, with everything seemingly moving its way, campaign finance reform remains stymied in Washington. Republicans and Democrats have each tried to skew the rules to their own advantage and resisted compromise. By carefully including elements that have public relations appeal in their proposed packages, both parties have attempted to portray themselves as the champions of the public interest. In the process, the public interest lobby itself has proven to be ineffective at balancing party concerns and appears misinformed about the role money plays in modern election campaigns.

Through all the deliberations recounted in this chapter, the focus is entirely on reform of senatorial and congressional campaigns, and, with the exception of soft money and contribution limits, the discussion has little or no direct reference to the problems pertaining to presidential campaigns—as noted in Chapters 2 and 3.

PREVIOUS REFORM EFFORTS

Election reform was a charm issue in the 1970s. The Federal Election Campaign Act was enacted in 1971, strengthened in the wake of Watergate in 1974, and fine-tuned in response to Supreme Court doctrine in 1976. Additional amendments passed in 1979 were designed to rejuvenate the role of party organizations in the electoral process.

Since that time, no attempts to adjust the federal election process have been enacted. The Republican ascension to the White House and majority status in the Senate following the 1980 elections put the reform movement into a state that, if not dead, was at least comatose. Reform reemerged in 1986, when Boren and Senator Barry M. Goldwater (R–AZ) offered a bill that would have curbed the total amount of PAC money a member could accept. The effort to set aggregate limits elicited favorable comment on and off Capitol Hill, but it failed to draw conclusive action before Congress adjourned.

Strengthened in revision, the Boren proposal returned as Senate Bill 2 (S 2) after the Democrats regained control of the Senate following the 1986 elections. Cosponsored by an enthusiastic majority leader, Robert Byrd, and all but ten members of the Democratic Caucus, S 2 was placed on a fast track. A new version of the bill—now loaded with new reforms—cleared the Senate Committee on Rules and Administration by a strictly partisan vote of 8 to 3 on April 29, 1987.

The new bill provided for a general election public financing system to assist those senatorial candidates who chose to observe spending limits in primary and general elections and who raised a minimum amount from individual contributions—the precise levels depending upon the voting-age population of the state. Those candidates who received public funding would have been required to accept no more than 20 percent of their total primary and general election funds from PACs. The bill also set an aggregate limit on PAC funds that noncomplying candidates could receive, amounting to 30 percent of the state's primary spending limit. Other prescribed restrictions included aggregate limits on national party committee receipt of PAC contributions, prohibition of the bundling of contributions by PACs or their connected organizations, and broadened disclosure requirements to ensure the reporting of certain kinds of soft money expenditures.[4]

The goal of the Byrd-Boren bill was to decrease the dependence of candidates on PAC contributions. But if enacted, it might have had several unintended consequences. The diminution of PAC influence would have shifted the relationships between candidates and PACs by changing their funding strategies. Faced with a finite amount to be raised from such sources, campaigns would tend to seek out only high-budget PACs, filling their quotas with a minimum of effort. Smaller PACs would be uncompetitive and would likely be neglected by all but the more struggling candidates.

The aggregate limit provision in Byrd-Boren was a new concept, not to be found anywhere in federal law. Had it became law, the courts almost certainly would have been confronted with new problems of definition, perhaps resulting in more legal upheaval.

MISCONCEPTIONS AND MISCALCULATIONS

In proposing both public financing and spending limits in S 2, the Democrats at once alienated needed Republican support and gave their opponents the cover with which to withstand pressures for reform. Although the Supreme Court's 1976 decision in *Buckley* v. *Valeo* had clearly made incentives like public financing a necessary step in the establishment of effective expenditure ceilings, the rationale of such limits seemed strained in light of recent evidence. The 1986 election returns offered little correlation between expenditure levels and electoral success for a majority of the 15 biggest-spending candidates lost, and 5 challengers beat incumbents who had spent twice as much. Moreover, the Democratic capture of the Senate—conjoined with a continuing control of the House—put Republicans in a mood to seek to stop limits at any price. Cognizant of the fact that their own candidates tended to raise funds more easily than their Democratic counterparts and determined to reverse their minority status, Republican leaders decried spending limits as a form of incumbent protection. They pointed to the enormous advantages of incumbency—high name recognition, franked mailings, access to free media exposure—and declared that large expenditures provided the only means by which challengers could level the playing field.

To gain the upper hand in the contest for public support, Republicans used the bill's public finance provisions to deride it as another raid on the treasury by free-spending, free-loading Democratic politicians. Senator Bob Packwood (R–OR) led the attack, declaring that S 2 was an attempt by Democrats "to take three or four hundred million dollars from taxpayers . . . to perpetuate their majority in the U.S. Congress, period."[5] Democrats countered that proposals such as the one offered by Packwood to ban PACs from congressional races altogether were a "smoke-screen" designed to rechannel PAC dollars through the party committee structure—a Republican strong point.[6]

At a June 10, 1987, caucus, the Republican Conference voted not to accept any public financing or spending limit provisions.[7] It was a Rubicon crossing that did not lack in ironies: Senator Ted Stevens (R–AK), ranking Republican member of the Senate Rules Committee, found himself leading a filibuster against voluntary expenditure limits while cosponsoring a constitutional amendment that would allow them to be mandatory; and Senate Minority Leader Robert Dole criticized public financing for senatorial campaigns while planning to seek public funds for his presidential bid.[8]

Despite personal conflicts, the party line was a predictable, pragmatic exercise. As National Republican Senatorial Committee counsel Benjamin

Ginsberg explained to the *New York Times,* "Republicans have taken the time and money to build a much larger fund-raising base."[9] Public financing could reduce that advantage, just as spending limits could undermine Republican prospects of overcoming the advantage members of the Democratic majority enjoy as incumbents.[10] Given the polarity between party positions on spending limits, no grounds for compromise were apparent.

Accordingly, S 2 traveled a rocky road from its introduction as it struggled along the legislative process with little semblance of bipartisan support. Party lines defied defection as no more than two Republicans cosponsored the bill in its various revisions, and no more than three supported it in the eight cloture votes called in its behalf by Majority Leader Byrd. Only two Democratic senators failed to cosponsor or vote for cloture. In the end, neither the original substitute made by the Rules and Administration Committee nor various other reincarnations of Byrd-Boren managed to overcome a determined Republican filibuster.

Provisions of S 2 that started out offering participating candidates a block public funding grant of up to 80 percent of the general election spending limit gradually dwindled in successive revisions to 40 percent, then to matching funds, and eventually to an "insurance policy" that would provide public funding only if a candidate's opponent exceeded the voluntary expenditure limit. The bill was revised so often its nickname became the "Boren Again Bill", as different parts of the proposal kept springing back to life in new form.

Support for S 2 from the public interest lobby remained strong throughout the bill's many lives. Some 430 newspaper editorials—including influential entries from the *New York Times* and the *Washington Post*—endorsed the bill, as did 73 organizations.[11] The most powerful of these, Common Cause, had made public financing the cornerstone of much of its rhetoric on the reform issue but continued to back the measure even after such provisions were stripped from it or greatly diluted. Support from the reformers and the media would sway few votes, however, unless S 2 could rally some noticeable support from Republicans.

Such a breakthrough appeared to be at hand in early June when Senator Boren reported that now-retired Senator Goldwater had come on board. As the "grand old man" of the GOP, Goldwater's endorsement could have provided cover for several wavering Republicans, but it collapsed under apparent pressure from the Senate minority leadership: In a few days, Republicans were able to announce that the former presidential nominee had withdrawn his support from S 2 after learning it included public financing provisions, unlike the 1986 version he had cosponsored.[12]

With direct public financing proving to be an insurmountable stumbling block, the Democrats began to float some innovative alternatives that may eventually find their way into law in some form. The Senate Rules Committee version of S 2 would have given candidates who agreed to voluntary spending limits the privilege of buying nonpreemptible broadcast time at the lowest advertising rate offered to a station's commercial clients. One of Byrd's compromises (borrowed from the HR 2464 proposal of House Elections Subcommittee Chair Al Swift) provided 30 percent discounts on broadcast advertising and 25 percent discounts on postal mailing rates. Nonparticipating candidates also were required to advertise their noncompliance with spending limits.[13]

Republicans found this last provision particularly worrisome because of its coercive effect, and though a few might have voted for the indirect subsidies had they not been tied to limits, the stalemate continued.

CHARADES

In February 1988, reform prospects brightened briefly when negotiating teams of four senators from each party sat down to work out a compromise. Hopes ran high after Assistant Minority Leader Alan Simpson (R–NY) prefaced the meeting by claiming he was willing to "put everything on the table" if the Democrats did the same: "If they will get serious with us on soft money and in-kind contributions," he proclaimed on February 17, "we will get serious with them on taxpayer financing and limiting PACs."[14]

But the move toward accord fell apart shortly thereafter over the issue of spending limits, which had become the lightning rod for Republican opposition once the public funding portion of S 2 had been whittled down. "We could have passed what could have added up to a significant piece of campaign-finance reform," reported negotiator Mitch McConnell (R–KY). "It was the spending limits that broke down the process."[15] Democrats offered to include a formula to adjust state-by-state limits to account for historical dominance by one party—such as the Democratic advantage in the South—but Republicans still balked.

In the midst of a late February effort by Senate Democrats to embarrass their Republican adversaries with three days of round-the-clock sessions, Senator Packwood made history by being forcibly carried into the Senate chambers by the sergeant at arms. The Republicans' strategy had stymied the designs of Majority Leader Byrd by having only one of their members present, in effect requiring a quorum call for each vote. Forced to rely on his own troops to come up with the fifty-one bodies needed to keep the Senate in session, the frustrated Byrd ordered that minority members be arrested on sight and brought to the floor. The resulting

Packwood incident—however humorous—spoiled the atmosphere, leading such potential Republican allies of reform as Arlen Specter of
Pennsylvania to characterize the dramatic act as the "tyranny of the
majority leader."[16]

With partisanship now implacably hardened, the final of eight cloture
attempts on S 2 occurred February 28, 1988, and failed by a 51 to 42
margin. The best showing the bill had achieved was 5 votes short of
the 60 needed to cut off debate.

THE CONSTITUTIONAL APPROACH

With S 2 finally handed to him, Senator Byrd moved up SJ Res 282,
a constitutional amendment offered by Senator Ernest Hollings (D–SC)
that would have enabled the Senate to impose spending limits without
forcing candidates into acceptance of public funding.

At this point, a few Republicans were on record as favoring spending
limits but opposing public financing, and the Hollings approach therefore
seemed likely to garner more support than Byrd-Boren. Although it
would need a larger vote to pass—a constitutional amendment requires
a two-thirds majority to pass instead of the three-fifths required by a
filibustered bill such as S 2—the need to override an almost certain
presidential veto of the Byrd-Boren legislation made either outcome
problematic. The Hollings resolution could not clear the cloture bar
either, though it came close. An initial failure of 53 to 37 was encouraging
for head counters tallied six of the missing ten senators as favoring
cloture. However, a second and final attempt on April 22, 1988, failed
as well.

The objective of the proposed amendment was to neutralize principles
in *Buckley* v. *Valeo* that had invalidated the FECA's mandatory campaign
expenditure limits for federal candidates. Though the court ruled that
spending limits were unconstitutional, it said that if candidates accepted
public funds (or presumably other benefits) from the federal government,
they could be legally obligated to abide by "voluntary" limits as a
condition of their acceptance.

Hollings was highly critical of this Supreme Court decision, pointing
out that, during the 1920s, Senate winners had twice been denied their
seats on the basis of excessive campaign spending. Noting that the
Court upheld contribution limits because "the governmental interest
in preventing corruption" outweighs the free speech consideration,
Hollings wondered aloud why this same test would not apply to campaign
expenditures. Arguing that his resolution would restore the original
intent of the 1974 FECA amendments, the South Carolinian stated that

although "elections are supposed to be contests of ideas [instead] they degenerate into megadollar derbies."[17]

Some Democrats and Common Cause argued that the Hollings tactic would involve a long, arduous struggle through the state legislatures that would leave reform waiting for years—and still leave the spending limits to be enacted.[18] The added flexibility of not having to preface limits with the offering of public finance seems to have had surprisingly limited appeal. Few senators favored one and not the other—even as freestanding concepts independent of any merging.

THE CLIMATE SHIFTS

The 1987–1988 debate over campaign finance reform was fueled primarily by Republican concerns about the seeming irreversibility of their minority status and by reformers' alarm over the growing presence of lobbyists in campaign finance. Commentary from the press was largely muted; few members of Congress felt constituent pressure on the matter or regarded it as a campaign issue. That was soon to change: Several events that unfolded over the following two years brought public opinion to bear on the finance reform question with an intensity that had been missing since the Watergate scandal of 1973–1974.

First, the presidential campaign fund-raisers openly disclosed their $100,000 contributors during the 1988 general election race, as noted in Chapter 3. Many journalists and opinion leaders were taken aback; they had assumed that the reforms of the 1970s had driven such large contributors underground, if not out of the federal campaign system altogether. For many, it was a rude introduction to the system of "soft money" that had been introduced by the FECA amendments of 1979 and increasingly spawned a class of elite fund-raisers during the 1980s. The practice allowed contributors to avoid federal limits when they donated to state or local party activities not directly related to a federal campaign, a scheme that so offended the sensibilities of editorial writers that the staid *New York Times* started to call soft money "sewer money."

The 1989 collapse of the savings and loan industry—with its bailout tab of several hundred billion dollars, as noted in Chapter 5—set off a hunt for government scapegoats that quickly found its way to the door of federal campaign finance. It was revealed that in April 1987, a group of five U.S. senators met with regulators from the Home Loan Bank Board at the request of Arizona developer Charles Keating. Pointed questions were raised about a year-long investigation of Keating's Lincoln Savings and Loan. Washington subsequently overrode the regional office's decision to close the thrift, but Keating's empire soon collapsed, creating a taxpayer liability of $2 billion. The "Keating Five" had received $1.3

million in contributions from the fallen financier, funneled either to their campaigns or PACs or soft money projects with which they were associated.[19] Other less dramatic episodes surfaced involving favor-trading between lawmakers and savings and loan operators, and strong correlations were drawn between industry contributions and favorable votes, most notably in a study by Common Cause that drew criticism from numerous members of Congress.[20]

Though the savings and loan scandal was slow to develop and even slower to attract public attention, the 101st Congress elicited an immediate negative response when it attempted to raise its pay in its opening session. Led by consumer advocate Ralph Nader and columnist Jack Anderson and exhorted by dozens of radio talk show hosts, a populist revolt inundated Capitol Hill with threatening communications. With each body left to set its own compensation, the House withdrew to the more modest position of a 25 percent raise tied to the prohibition of honoraria, while the Senate retreated on salary but not on honoraria. Despite this seeming contrition, evidence suggests many voters took the whole affair as confirmation that their elected representatives were becoming increasingly less responsive to their wishes.[21]

This theme dovetailed nicely with disturbing evidence emanating from the 1988 elections: Of the six House incumbents defeated for reelection in November, only one had not been tainted by scandal. According to the Congressional Research Service, the reelection rate was the highest in 198 years. Only one incumbent in seven failed to exceed the landslide margin of 60 percent of the vote.[22] Incumbents also took in about six times more PAC money than their challengers[23]— a sea change from eight years earlier, when the ratio was only 2.4 to 1.[24] A consensus among opinionmakers began to form, one that ascribed an alleged congressional invulnerability and devotion to special interests to a political finance system dominated by lobbyists backed by PAC contributions.

The Bush administration seized the opportunity presented by this climate to advocate a radically restrictive restructuring of the system. Released in June 1989, the Bush proposals were predictably partisan, calling for the emasculation of PACs (which had directed 62 percent of their 1988 contributions to Democrats) and enhancing the role of party committees (which had been more fruitful for Republicans, by a ratio of 3 to 1). This White House effort was soon tranformed into a twenty-five-point program for reform presented by the House minority leadership in September 1989.

This Republican plan was particularly noteworthy in that it sought to shut off or severely curtail several sources of campaign funding while making few provisions for increasing revenue from other directions.

Its adoption *in toto* would surely have resulted in lower-profile campaigns, a curious goal for a minority party determined to keep spending lids off. Among other things, it would

- Reduce the allowable PAC contribution to an individual candidate from $5,000 to $1,000 per election—despite the fact that the original limits had been set when the dollar was worth nearly three times its current value,
- Prohibit the bundling of campaign contributions by corporate, union, or trade association PACs—maintaining the privilege only for ideological and party committees,
- Forbid candidates to maintain their own PACs—a practice used to greatest effect by the majority with its leadership PACs,
- Require union members to approve in advance any portion of dues withheld for political activities—moneys that have been contributed to Democratic candidates by a 12 to 1 ratio,
- Ban all soft money contributions to national parties as well as those given to state parties for use in federal elections—both practices that are widely thought to lend disproportionate benefit to Democrats, and
- Lift all limits upon political parties' contributions to candidates, other than in a contested primary—a move that would unleash the Republican advantage in party fund-raising.[25]

THE SEARCH FOR CONSENSUS

With the public interest lobby insisting on comprehensive election reform and the Republicans now pushing a different type of reform, the majority leadership on Capitol Hill had little choice but to put the issue high on the agenda of the 101st Congress. Speaker Jim Wright (D–WA) and Minority Leader Robert Michel (R–IL) appointed a House Bipartisan Task Force for Campaign Reform, but its members quickly deadlocked on all major issues.[26]

Senate Minority Leader Dole suggested to Majority Leader George Mitchell (D–ME) that they try an end around to break the partisan legislative impasse that had characterized previous task force negotiations. On February 8, 1990, they appointed a bipartisan Senate Campaign Finance Reform Panel, consisting of lawyers and academics with election issue expertise, and charged it with using its detached perspective to find the avenues of compromise that had eluded senators. The new ad hoc body was directed to concern itself only with rules to govern U.S. Senate campaigns and to report back within a month.

In addition to the senior author of this book, members of the panel included Jan Baran and Robert F. Bauer, respective counsels to the Republican and Democratic senatorial campaign committees; Richard Moe, a former Democratic state chair and longtime aide to former vice president Walter Mondale; David Magleby of Brigham Young University, coauthor of *The Money Chase: Congressional Campaign Finance Reform;* and Larry Sabato of the University of Virginia, author of *PAC Power: Inside the World of Political Action Committees.*

Submitted on March 6, the panel's recommendations were released at a press conference the following day. Majority Leader Mitchell hailed the report as a "breakthrough" and expressed hope that the "report will serve to advance the debate and accelerate the time in which we have meaningful campaign finance reform." Perhaps in response to the semblance of spending limits present in the proposal, Minority Leader Dole was more guarded in his enthusiasm, calling the development a "potential breakthrough." A joint statement by the leaders said the study "shows the issue is capable of being resolved despite the strong differences between Republicans and Democrats."[27]

By staying focused on the public interest in campaign finance reform while maintaining a balance of partisan concerns, the panel succeeded in crafting a package that had both political appeal and practicality. The critical provisions dealt with a scheme for "reasonably high" and "flexible" voluntary spending limits that avoided the stumbling block of direct public financing. The particulars covered a wide range of innovations:

- Voluntary expenditure limits would be set high enough for challengers to achieve a level of recognition among the electorate comparable to that enjoyed by incumbents and would vary according to the population of each state; however, the limits would be made flexible by exempting in-state contributions made by individuals up to a certain level.
- Candidate incentives to abide by the limits would include postal discounts, reduced broadcast rates, and a 100 percent tax credit for any in-state individual taxpayer contributing to the campaign.
- The $1,000 limit on individual contributions would be raised modestly, then be indexed for inflation.
- Bundling by corporate and union PACs and registered lobbyists would be prohibited. Permissible bundled donations would be fully disclosed, along with any expenses incurred in the process.
- Parties would be given eight hours of free time per year by all broadcasters, including guaranteed prime-time and preelection slots. Party expenditures for such efforts as research and get-out-the-vote

and voter registration drives would be subject to "generous allow-
ances," if not held beyond restriction altogether.

- Soft money would be clearly divided between state and federal
  campaign funds and completely disclosed at all levels. More substantive restrictions would be applied to soft money activities such
  as voter contact, campaign overhead, fund-raising, and shared
  broadcast media.
- Political action committees would have the size of their permissible
  contributions cut in half once the candidate's PAC receipts exceeded
  one-third of the spending limit. PACs would be prohibited from
  making postelection debt retirement contributions to Senate victors
  for the first two years of the ensuing term.[28]

A common thread in the plan was the determination to expand
selectively rather than restrict the resources available to campaigns,
raising the profile of races to make citizens—particularly home state
contributors—more active in the process and incumbents more responsive to the public will. PAC money, for example, though assessed
by the report as a more interested form of giving than contributions
from individuals or party organizations, was only lightly discouraged.
Its influence would have been reduced, however, by the effect of various
incentives to encourage other campaign sources.

The delicate treatment of the PAC issue represented one of several
balancing acts the panel proposal performed between conflicting partisan interests: Republicans, who received only 38 percent of PAC money
and wanted it eliminated, got its influence reduced; Democrats, most
of whom wanted PACs maintained, got their wish—albeit with reduced
circumstances. Other crucial balances were struck on spending limits
and their inducements. Limits would be established—for Democrats—
but left with a narrow escape hatch for Republicans. Democrats would
get communications grants and discounts for their underfunded challengers and open-seat contenders, and the Republicans garnered increased party participation and some union restraints.

At first, it appeared the panel might have opened the way to significant
reform. Partisan Senators David Boren and Mitch McConnell both
expressed enthusiasm for the report and its prospects of being largely
enacted.[29] Numerous newspaper editorials and op-ed columns endorsed
the findings, and Common Cause praised them as a formula that "could
open the door for serious bipartisan negotiations," although it termed
the treatment of soft money as "fundamentally flawed."[30]

Meanwhile, almost as if on cue, the latest edition of "Boren Again"—
now numbered S 137—was reported out of the Senate Rules Committee
the day after the panel report was released. The seven-minute meeting

produced a 7 to 3 vote split along party lines, a predictable result given that the Democrats were basically coming back to where they had left off on the issue in 1988, their proposed legislation having changed little. The Rules Committee chairman, Wendell Ford (D–KY), conceded that the bill—as then constituted—signified little more than his party's vehicle for negotiations to be conducted by the Senate leaders, a signal that the committee was effectively being bypassed. Such a novel approach had recently been used with great success, breaking a long-standing deadlock over a clean air bill.[31]

Departures from the panel blueprint for compromise began almost immediately, though both parties would eventually include many of its ideas for their competing proposals, each seeking the mantle of legitimate reform. The *Washington Times* reported that Republicans were delighted at the "flexible limits" proposal, regarding it as "no overall spending limit at all."[32] Already leery of the fact that the concept of a nonpartisan expert panel had first been suggested by Senator Dole, Democrats began to balk at the idea of limit flexibility, claiming that it would not end the "money chase" that remained the primary source of motivation for reform among individual senators.[33]

But the Republicans had their own qualms about the report (primarily because it trod lightly on PACs and soft money) and were in fact already plotting a strategy to use the legislative issue as a public relations vehicle. "The goal here of Republicans is to get to the issue of the source of the money," a Republican senator confided at the time. "When you look at who is more reliant on different sources of money, the Republicans have been much more reliant on individual contributions and party activities, and the Democrats as a party have relied much more heavily on political action committee donations and out-of-state contributions. We think this is something the public has never understood—and won't like."[34]

DESCENT INTO SPECTACLE

Partisan suspicions and political gamesmanship began to threaten the "breakthrough" opportunity presented by the panel report. The window of opportunity seemed narrow. And as the November election drew nearer, partisan feelings intensified. Yet, at various intervals over the next few months, it appeared action was imminent.

The first real concession in the partisan deadlock occurred on April 20, when the Democratic Caucus voted to accept the concept of exempting small in-state contributions from the spending limits. The gambit was a significant concession to Republicans and appeared to bring S 137 largely in line with the Mitchell-Dole panel report, but by now the Republicans had their own alternative bill and had set a game plan into full swing. "It's not in the bill I've been shopping around," responded Republican point man Mitch McConnell about the new flexibility in the Democrats' proposed limits. "I don't find much [GOP] sympathy for that. We don't think it's helpful to Republicans."[35]

This was in marked contrast to the Kentuckian's assessment of the concept when it had been unveiled as part of the panel package six weeks earlier. "There is widespread enthusiasm among Republicans" for avoiding absolute limits by restricting out-of-state money, McConnell had then declared. "There's no limit on good money from those who can vote for you in your state. That's why we're excited."[36] Such an apparent change in posture invited skepticism about the Republicans' commitment to reform from such observers as the *Washington Post,* which accused them of "stonewalling."[37]

The Boren bill called for general election expenditure limits ranging between $950,000 and $5.5 million, based on a state's voting-age population. (Primary election limits expanded the total figure 67 percent, up to a maximum of $2,750,000; the Democratic in-state donor exemption—once incorporated—was limited to individual contributions of $100 or less and given a cap of 25 percent of the general election spending limit. Presuming a fully utilized exemption, the full limit range was $1.8 million to $9.6 million.)

A study released on May 17 by the Committee for the Study of the American Electorate (CSAE) appeared to support the Republican contention that limits set at the S 137 levels would amount to enhanced incumbent protection. Of the 32 Senate challengers elected in the previous four election cycles, CSAE found that 14 would have exceeded the S 137 limits, even after applying a full 25 percent supplement for in-state contributions of $100 or less. Moreover, though the spending figures had been adjusted for inflation as measured by the Consumer Price Index, CSAE director Curtis Gans pointed out that campaign costs had actually risen at a much sharper rate. One indication was the fact that, while the CPI had doubled between 1978 and 1990, Senate campaign expenditures had increased by six and one-half times.[38] Common Cause disputed the CSAE conclusions, releasing its own study, which indicated that had S 137 been in place for the 1988 elections with every candidate abiding by the limits, challengers would have gained $21.7 million in campaign funds, and incumbents would have lost $23.6 million.[39]

Through late April and into May, Senate Democrats continued to debate their differences in caucus, trying to reach a party consensus on S 137 before it moved to the floor. Periodically, they would announce developments such as the in-state contribution exemption, in effect releasing trial balloons and noting how far they would fly. Mitchell and Boren faced considerable consternation within their own ranks, led principally by the Democratic National Committee and the 11 Senate Democrats facing their first reelection campaigns in 1992.

DNC Chairman Ron Brown was critical of the Boren bill's soft money provisions: applying federal limits to what state parties can spend on generic party activities such as get-out-the-vote drives and voter contact—in effect hardening soft money and eliminating most of its usefulness as a federal campaign cash conduit. The Democratic party structure had only recently become proficient at exploiting the soft money provision purposefully opened by the 1979 FECA amendments and had just launched an ambitious plan for coordinated campaigns in more than a dozen states, to be fueled in part by soft money.[40]

The freshman Democrats up in 1992 were already facing a tough fight. Most were upset victors; counting open seats, 9 of them had won election by less than 6 percentage points, and 5 triumphed by less than 2 points.[41] Most represented conservative states; with President Bush's popularity at a record high, they faced the possibility of long Republican coattails. Meanwhile, most Democrats were well on their way toward raising money up to S 137's spending limits and had already spent some of it; their Republican opponents had not gotten started yet and would be in a position to concentrate more spending and possibly to outspend them through the campaign's critical late stages. The Republicans opposed the aggregate PAC contribution limits in the Boren bill (which ranged between $190,950 and $825,000) and the premium on small, in-state contributions; several Republican incumbents had been very successful in attracting big money in small amounts from out-of-state in the past campaigns. With the easiest money these senators could collect curtailed, they could expect little or no relief from the distraction of having to run back home on a regular basis to seek in-state funds that, in small states at least, might be inadequate for expensive campaigns.

After the Republican alternative bill (S 2595) was unveiled on May 1—its potential boosted by its call for the elimination of PACs—Mitchell made a switch. The Democratic Caucus agreed to a new provision banning PAC contributions to Senate candidates but resurrected the plan for nearly full public financing. In effect, it was a major Democratic move dedicated to political posturing on campaign finance reform; it would not be the last. By having their own bill essentially ban PACs from Senate campaigns, then making the package totally unacceptable to Republicans by calling for substantial and direct public financing, the Democrats tried to turn the tables and make the Republicans appear as the defenders of PACs and the enemies of reform. They further fostered this impression by expanding the expenditure limits of S 137 by roughly 50 percent and incorporating the $100 in-state exemption (albeit with a cap amounting to 25 percent of the base limit).

Despite this maneuver, the Democratic bill put many Senate Democrats—particularly the 1986 class and those from small states—on a sharp edge, fearing that they might actually get what they were now loudly wishing for. PACs had supplied 38 percent of Democratic incumbent receipts in the last cycle (nearly three times the proportion received by Republican challengers) and Caucus members demanded to know where they could make up the shortfall. Small-state senators, such as Max Baucus (D–MT), were particularly up in arms because they were especially dependent on PACs and out-of-state money (which the bill sought to deemphasize). The national parties, already wielding an enormous influence in small-state elections with their strategic infusions of last-minute cash, would be even further enhanced. It appeared to many Democratic senators that they were playing to the Republicans' strength.

A Caucus revolt soon erupted, determined to add an unlimited exemption to the S 137 limits, available only to incumbents. The rebel proposal amounted to legalizing open-ended incumbent "slush" funds similar to the one that embroiled Richard Nixon in the "Checkers scandal" of 1952. Raised from private funds and exempt from expense account limits as well as campaign fund restrictions, the provision covered "costs of any ordinary and necessary expenses incurred in connection with an individuals's duties as a . . . United States Senator." Recognizing that the addition of this clause to the bill would forfeit the moral high ground of reform to the Republicans, Mitchell, Boren, and Senator Joe Biden (D–DE) succeeded in pressuring their colleagues into a compromise: The special incumbent funds would be limited to 15 percent of a candidate's total spending limit or $300,000, whichever was lower. A grandfather clause exempting money raised before passage of the bill also was added.[42]

The alternative bills finally came to the floor for debate on May 11 but were promptly sent to a negotiation panel of eight senators, equally divided between the parties. Senators Boren and McConnell—authors of the rival bills—were designated team leaders. Democrats joining them were Democratic Senatorial Campaign Committee (DSCC) chair John Breaux (LA), class of 1986 member Tom Daschle (SD), and John Kerry (MA), spokesman of the Caucus rebels; other Republicans were National Republican Senatorial Committee (NRSC) chair Don Nickles (OK), Bob Packwood (OR), and Warren Rudman (NH). Because these appointees were among the party partisans on the campaign finance reform issue, their prospects for finding a successful settlement did not appear to be promising.[43]

Negotiators opened their sessions on May 22 and quickly found some common ground on several fronts:[44]

- Providing candidates with reduced rates on broadcast advertising. Both bills called for requiring broadcast stations to sell non-preemptible time to candidates at the lowest unit rate, beginning forty-five days before the primary. The Democratic bill would have kept the rule in place throughout the general election period, the Republicans' bill only for the last sixty days. Democrats also would have restricted the privilege to those complying with their spending limits.
- Prohibiting the bundling of contributions by PACs, unions, corporations, trade associations, or their representatives. Republicans wanted party committees exempted; Democrats did not.
- Restricting the use of personal funds in excess of $250,000. Spending more than that amount would have disqualified a candidate from receiving public funding under the Democratic plan; Republicans wanted to give the opponents of such big personal spenders a boost in the individual contribution limit to $5,000 per election, up from the usual $1,000.
- Curbing independent expenditure campaigns. The Democratic bill called for providing public funds to candidates attacked by campaigns operating independently of a candidate committee. The Republicans sought only wider disclosure of their activities.
- Toughening the Federal Election Commission. Both bills called for shortening the time periods of FEC action, increasing the minimum penalties for violation of the FECA, and authorizing the FEC to seek court injunctions. In preliminary procedures, such as decisions to investigate violations, Democrats wanted to make the recommendation of the commission general counsel sustainable by three commissioners, in effect giving the counsel a vote on such matters.

Despite the many goals shared by the parties, the finance reform negotiations broke down on July 14 after five meetings, stalemated over spending limits. "I don't think there's any point in having any more meetings," Republican Senator McConnell said. "We've had an opportunity to work out a bill, but they wanted it their way or not at all." Boren hinted that the ambitious public funding provisions in S 137 were readily negotiable and might be sacrificed entirely but declared, "We could not yield on the question of putting a limit on overall spending because it is the essence for reform."[45] Democrats justified their intransigence by comparing campaign finance to the arcade game of "Whack-a-Mole"—knock down special interest money in one area and it will merely rise up in another. This also is known as the "pop-up" theory. The only way to control it, they claimed ironically, was to limit overall spending.

Although the excessive public financing levels in Boren's bill at this point may have reflected a negotiating stance, they seemed daunting to the Republican team. Candidates would have been provided with 70 percent of the general election spending limit in government funds after raising only a tenth of that limit with contributions of $250 or less (at least half of it from in-state sources). Additional subsidies to be provided to complying candidates included a 75 percent reduction on first-class mail costs, substantial discounts on third-class mail, and vouchers for television advertising amounting to 20 percent of the general election expenditure limit. In effect, once the candidate had fulfilled the task of raising the qualifying contributions, the government would foot the other 90 percent of the general election bill—not counting the 25 percent supplement the campaign could seek from low-dollar donors back home.

The televison vouchers could only have been spent on ads of one to five minutes in length, an attempt to encourage the use of messages more substantive than the usual thirty-second spot announcement. This effort to control the tenor of campaign dialogue drew its inspiration from the Danforth-Hollings "Clean Campaign Act," a bill unsuccessfully floated in the previous two congresses. Another S 137 provision with similar ancestry called for candidates to personally appear at the end of each of their ads, acknowledging responsibility.

Judging from the public dialogue, the Republicans appeared to be willing to accept the postal subsidies but no additional taxpayer largesse; the Democrats might have accommodated those sentiments but not without pointing out their sacrifice. The focus then became the spending limits set forth in S 137, from which the Democrats would not budge even with PAC restrictions as part of the package. Some Republicans might have been persuaded to endorse limits that were set substantially higher than those in the Democratic bill and indexed to something more reliable than the Consumer Price Index, which has historically expanded far less than actual campaign costs.[46]

An upward adjustment in their proposed limits would have been in the Democrats' interest once most of the politically unpopular public finance incentives had been jettisoned; the pressures for many candidates to compete outside the strictures might otherwise have been too great. Where to draw the line would have been a major sticking point, however: Republicans were bound to press for at least the CSAE suggestion of

$1.50 per eligible voter, a figure based on the average expenditure of successful House candidates in the 1988 cycle. Even adjusted downward in the larger states, such levels were without doubt too rich for the Democrats. Using the median-sized state of Colorado as a benchmark, the CSAE method would have set a limit 93 percent higher than S 137.

There were other, lesser conflicts to resolve, such as the emphasis on new soft money restrictions. Boren and Mitchell had succeeded in placing measures into the Democratic bill that would virtually repeal the 1979 FECA amendments, public policy that was finally beginning to achieve its objective of strengthening the state party organizations with "big money" donations. By contrast, the Republicans' fire was concentrated on soft money generated by nonparty committees, especially that used by labor unions.

None of these differences, however, seems insurmountable in retrospect—fueling speculation that the Democrats' real departure from the negotiating process had been signaled when they embraced the abolition of PAC money. They seemed never able to retreat from that line in the sand, nor could they advance beyond it.

DISRUPTIVE HOUSE PARTIES

With the seeming failure of the negotiating process in the Senate, the focus of the debate shifted back to the House, where members had largely ignored the issue of campaign finance since their own failure at bipartisanship in the fall of 1989. Perhaps because members of the lower chamber were more dependent on PAC contributions than their colleagues in the Senate, action there was characterized by far less ambitious reform and a more determined pursuit of partisan interest. There was never any doubt that its final product would be sharply divided along party lines.

House Republicans introduced ten separate bills (de facto amendments) on June 13, each calling for a complementary set of reforms—such as cutting the maximum contribution a PAC could make to candidates by 80 percent and requiring that half of a candidate's money be raised from constituents—but quickly got nowhere with the majority leadership.

In an attempt to avoid being tagged as obstructionist, House Democrats shifted gears in late June. Representative Al Swift (D–WA), chairman of the House Elections Subcommittee and head of the Campaign Reform Task Force, abruptly altered his long-standing, modest, and simple proposal to limit House spending to $550,000, no more than half of which could be raised from PACs. The new Swift plan—quickly endorsed by House Speaker Tom Foley—called for a sliding-scale approach in governing how much individual PACs could give to candidates. "Small-donor committees"—defined as those that accepted no more than $240 per year from each of their contributors—could continue to give candidates $5,000 per election if they boasted a membership of more than 10,000 (mainly labor unions and certain membership organizations); those with 5,000–10,000 members could give only $2,500; those with fewer than 5,000 members would be limited to giving $1,500. Committees that took in contributions of more than $240 ($20 per month on a union checkoff) would be held to the same $1,000 limit that restrained individuals.

This revamped plan floated by the House Democratic leadership (HR 5400) was roundly criticized from all directions. The $550,000 limit was nearly $100,000 less than the average expenditure of successful 1988 House challengers, leading critics to categorize it as an incumbent protection measure. The original $275,000 PAC limit would not have touched more than three-quarters of House incumbents in 1988, leaving room for nearly $33 million in PAC growth as against $8 million in losses from those who exceeded that level.[47] Though that stance already had the public interest lobby up in arms, the lack of an aggregate ceiling on a campaign's PAC donations sent it into a fury.

"The PAC proposal is a joke," insisted Common Cause president Fred Wertheimer. Joan Claybrook, head of Public Citizen, echoed those sentiments. "It treats the American people like fools," she said, adding that "it would not really take any money out of the system. I can't believe Democratic leaders would do this."[48] The reaction was a blow to the prestige of Swift and Foley, who had hitherto been regarded as allies of the reformers.[49]

Nor did the Swift action create any friendships among Republicans: Its provisions were clearly aimed at leaving labor PACs undisturbed while eviscerating those aligned with corporations, an unmistakably partisan tack. There was even considerable upset among Democrats when Representatives Mike Synar (OK), Dan Glickman (KS), and Dennis Eckart (OH) led a chorus of criticism from those determined to wear the mantle of reform in the fall campaign. Another faction in the Democratic Caucus complained loudly that the system had done well by the party and its incumbents and that there was little voter interest in reforming it. Emerging as the leader of this predominately urban antireform group was Robert Torricelli (D–NJ), a perennial designate for certain Democrats in partisan floor debates. "I do not see evidence of a public demand to alter the system along the lines I've seen presented," Torricelli insisted.[50] And although unfolding events would soon prove him wrong, his stand-pat faction would ultimately force concessions in the Democratic bill.

BURNED BY THE HOME FIRES

When Congress adjourned for the July 4 recess, it appeared no closer to producing successful legislation on campaign finance reform than when it had picked up the task nearly a year earlier. Time was growing short, and competition for attention would be felt from other top issues: civil rights, child care, crime, education, rights for the disabled, and housing among them. Given the intense personal interest members had in campaign reform, it would be a time-killer on the floor—a venue with almost no chance of producing a law. It appeared Majority Leader Mitchell might be compelled to let the issue die.

That outlook changed quickly when Congress reconvened in mid-July. The enormous tax burden being engineered by the savings and loan crisis had finally registered its weight with constituents. Members had gotten complaints while back home and were alarmed by reports from pollsters that their "reelect ratings" had almost uniformly plummeted ten points in the past month.[51] The Senate quickly penalized thrift leaders caught defrauding the taxpayers, voting 99 to 1 to imprison them. Then Congress turned its attention to the task of saving itself on the issue of campaign finance.

Common Cause had targeted 13 House incumbents for a lobby campaign at the grass roots, placing ads in major newspapers of their constituencies with such headlines as "S&L Interests Gave Members of Congress Millions" and "Taxpayers Were Ripped Off for Billions . . . And Congress Has Done Nothing."[52] The ads also made reference to the amount of PAC money the particular member had taken for recent campaigns, suggesting to the casual reader that they had been directly responsible for the savings and loan crisis. Wertheimer claimed the ad targets represented a "cross-section" of House members, but study of the group suggests the choices were more strategic: All 13 were influential Democrats who had accepted considerable amounts of PAC money.

The House Democratic leadership responded vociferously, vowing that Common Cause had overstepped its bounds and taken itself out of the debate over political finance reform.[53] Although the ad campaign exposed Common Cause as being somewhat hypocritical in the use of innuendo—a propaganda ploy they had earlier denounced—House Democrats soon restored the $275,000 aggregate PAC limit to their bill.

As July drew to a close with the floor debate on campaign reform only a week away, last-minute efforts at bipartisanship were attempted by the Senate leaders. Republican Senator Dole took another initiative by sending Democratic Senator Mitchell a letter outlining a proposal for spending limits so flexible the author referred to them as a series of "targets." Ceilings would be erected but only over money raised out of state from PACs and individual donations of more than $250.[54] Although minimal from the standpoint of limiting spending, the move was significant in that it put the Republicans on the record for the first time as being willing to accept some spending restraint on candidates. Such flexibility also was being hinted at by the House Republican leadership, with Minority Leader Bob Michel acknowledging, "I'll be the first to admit we're spending too much [on campaigns]."[55] During the floor debate a few days following Dole's letter, the *New York Times* reported that "a top Republican adviser said . . . if the ceiling [in the Democratic proposal] was raised by another $100,000 to $150,000 it might be acceptable to House Republicans."[56]

Despite the positive signals, the Senate Democratic Caucus rejected the Dole proposal on July 26. The following day, however, they agreed to accept the Republican provision to ban PACs altogether, backed up with a $1,000 limit on PAC contributions to candidates that would kick in if the total abolition were ruled unconstitutional—a highly unusual provision. Direct public financing also was stripped from the bill, with an exception made for candidates facing an opponent who refused to abide by the limits. McConnell termed this tactic "blatantly unconstitutional [because it] punished the candidate who exercises his First Amendment freedom."[57]

Given the voters' low opinion of PACs, the political unpopularity of public financing, and the Republicans' adamant opposition to the low spending limits in S 137, these responses suggest the Democrats had already resigned themselves to the inevitability of a presidential veto—indeed, they were now relying on it—and were beginning to craft the bill into campaign material for the fall campaign.

FLOOR COVERINGS

Intentions of political posturing were quickly confirmed in the action that began on the Senate floor July 30, continuing through three days of debate and sixteen roll call votes on amendments.

By a 77 to 23 vote, senators added an amendment offered by Christopher Dodd (D-CT) that called for the elimination of their honoraria allowance—medicine the House had taken the year before with the 25 percent pay raise. To prevent end runs around the ban, the measure called for limiting senators' outside earned income to 15 percent of their salaries. Upping the ante, Senator Daniel Patrick Moynihan (D-NY) offered a populist amendment which would have made unearned income (funds from investments) subject to the limit as well. Moynihan's amendment appeared doomed on a 49 to 49 tie when he jumped into the aisle, playfully pleading for "just one more vote." Senator Frank Murkowski (R–AK) obliged, and the amendment took its place among an array of S 137 public relations ornaments never intended to appear in law.

Two other such efforts came in the form of Republican amendments that Democrats felt compelled to support. One offered by Don Nickles (R–OK) would have barred the use of the senatorial franking privilege for mass mailings during an election year and prevented senators from lending portions of their franking budget to colleagues—a common cooperative practice designed to provide members with more mailings close to an election. The Nickles amendment also took aim at the House practice of exceeding its mailing budget by ordering the suspension of franking privileges once the annual budget had been exhausted. House members also were to be compelled to disclose the expense of their mail privilege exercises, a practice already observed by the Senate. Although the amendment was not a popular one among many senators, it passed with only a single dissenting vote.

Another surprise Republican victory was the adoption of an amendment proposed by Senator Pete Domenici (R–NM) that would limit out-of-state individual contributions to $250 per election. When Democratic colleagues complained that this development promised to hurt their fund-raising disproportionately, bill sponsor Boren cautioned: "I don't think you [should] expect that every amendment that passes will come out of conference."[58]

Other Republican amendments met a more expected fate. Senator McConnell's attempt to strip all public funding from the bill—including television time vouchers and postal discounts—appealed to a few fiscally conservative southern Democrats but still lost 46 to 49. Proponents had pointed to Congressional Budget Office estimates that pegged the bill's total subsidy costs at $56 million per cycle, arguing that such giveaways to politicians could hardly be justified in the face of a large budget deficit. Democrats were even less sympathetic to the attempt by Senator John McCain (R–AZ) to remove the $300,000 incumbent fund provision, beating it back 44 to 55. McCain had more success with his move to require candidates to use campaign contributions only for legitimate campaign activities and to remit any leftover funds to the treasury. A holdover from the original Bush proposals, this amendment would have been a major blow to incumbent security if applied to the House, where the common presence of large war chests was thought to be a prohibitive deterrent for potential challengers. Looking over its shoulder at a number of well-heeled congressmen, the Senate turned down the "zeroing-out" reform only on a tied 49 to 49 vote.

The Democratic bill was made to look more moderate by the 38 to 60 defeat of an amendment from John Kerry (D–MA) that would have extended direct public financing to all candidates at a level equal to 70 percent of the spending limit—in effect restoring the bill's original provisions. Kerry's proposal would have funded the public largesse with an additional $2 voluntary checkoff on individual income tax returns.[59] The idea so unsettled southern Democrats that Boren offered a sense of the Senate resolution that declared that the funds needed for the television vouchers, mail discounts, and contingency fund should come from FEC fines and voluntary contributions made by taxpayers from tax refunds—a tax add-on rather than a diversion of revenues with a tax checkoff. If these campaign fund revenues fell short of their obligations (as seems probable), payments to candidates would be prorated accordingly.[60] Republicans solidly opposed the measure, charging it was a Trojan horse designed to let tax revenues in through the back door at a later date. It passed on a 55 to 44 vote, split along party lines.

Concern over possible foreign influence in U.S. affairs was reflected in another successful amendment offered by Finance Committee Chairman Lloyd Bentsen (D–TX), which banned companies with majority foreign ownership from operating a political action committee. Although the measure would have been moot if the bill's provisions banning PACs altogether were declared unconstitutional, it was significant in that it gave a Senate endorsement to regulatory action being considered by the Federal Election Commission. According to a Congressional Research Service report issued in November 1989, 5 percent of corporate PAC contributions came from committees whose sponsoring company had "significant foreign ownership."[61]

Consideration of these various amendments proceeded smoothly, with a lack of rancor that was surprising in light of the tumultuous battles that had raged over the issue in the previous Congress. The Senate leadership assiduously avoided procedural stalemate in order to go on record as supporting campaign reform. Senators Mitchell and Dole, in effect, cut a deal: Democrats would not attempt to invoke cloture as long as Republicans moved their amendments without delay or filibuster.[62]

On August 1, Senator Dole began drawing the curtain on debate by presenting the Republicans' alternative bill. After it failed on a 44 to 55 party-line vote, the much-altered S 137 was passed 59 to 40. Five Republicans supported it: John McCain (AZ) and David Durenberger (MN), both countering ethics problems; the electorally embattled Larry Pressler (SD); and two moderate senators from New England, William Cohen (ME) and Jim Jeffords (VT). The only Democratic senator to oppose was Ernest Hollings (SC), still grumbling about public financing and advocating constitutional amendment. Response from the reformers was far more enthusiastic: "This is the most important step taken in the Congress since 1974 to deal with the enormous campaign finance problem," said Common Cause's Fred Wertheimer. "This will fundamentally change the system."[63]

A HOUSE DIVIDED

Reformers were markedly less pleased with the House version that passed two days later. Susan Lederman, president of the League of Women Voters, declared it was "dangerously close to being an incumbent protection bill," and Wertheimer dismissed it as "not real reform."[64] Representative Jim Leach (R–IA), a reform advocate, denounced the House action as a "sham and a shame."[65]

Already unpopular with the reform element for its deferential and partisan treatment of PACs, the Democrats' HR 5400 earned new status in those circles after its spending limits were loosened in a party caucus on August 1, just two days before the bill was scheduled to go to the floor on the eve of a month-long recess. Faced with opposition from representatives from the large urban "Rust Bowl" states, which faced considerable redistricting before the 1992 elections, Speaker Foley and Representative Swift agreed to a clause that would add $165,000 to a candidate's spending limit for the general election if he or she won the primary with less than two-thirds of the vote. Criminal penalties for candidates who exceeded the limits also were dropped, prohibitions on the use of soft money were loosened, and a ban on bundling by registered lobbyists was stricken.[66] As the last-minute party action took place behind closed doors, it was suspect.

It is ironic to note, however, that the most significant Caucus action taken—the flexible expansion of the bill's spending limits—was applauded as one that would increase the success rate for challengers. Still, the supplement would push the expenditure limit beyond the average amount laid out by successful challengers in 1988.

Spurred by their reflexive revulsion to political spending, the reformers and most editorialists quickly accepted the expertise of the victorious rebel congressmen and denounced the package of eleventh-hour adjustments as backsliding on reform. The contention was bolstered by reports filtering out of the Caucus that indicated many members wished to ditch the bill altogether. "People don't even want to think about competition," an anonymous Democratic congressman confided to the *Washington Post*: "These guys are paralyzed by change," said another. A third lawmaker offered an analysis that fairly encapsulates an explanation for all that had transpired in Congress over the issue: "The way it's going to work out is nothing is going to pass. Everyone has their fingers crossed that it will be vetoed by the president. The House doesn't want [campaign finance reform] to happen, the Senate doesn't want it to happen. They just want to get Common Cause and the editorial writers off their backs."[67]

Barely twenty-four hours before Congress was to adjourn for its August vacation, House Democratic leaders finished crafting a restrictive rule for the campaign finance debate that created much partisan enmity when it was rammed through the next day. Speaker Foley was far less accommodating to the minority than Senate Majority Leader Mitchell had been, entertaining no Republican amendments—only an up-or-down vote on their alternative reform package. As a means of appeasing reformer allies in the caucus, however, Foley permitted Mike Synar and David Obey (D–WI) to introduce an amendment calling for more strictures on PAC contributions, reduced individual donor limits, and up to $100,000 in public matching funds for House candidates. A sizable number of Democrats were opposed to these provisions, and Foley knew he could not muster the votes to pass them, but he agreed to give the reformers a chance to go on record as favoring measures more sweeping than those outlined in HR 5400. The move left an opening for the frustrated Republicans to exercise a parliamentary maneuver that nearly sank the bill.

Recognizing that Foley was counting on their votes to defeat the Synar-Obey amendment in order to keep it from costing the basic bill its majority, minority members declined to seek a roll call—as anticipated—when the amendment passed on a voice vote. An obscure emergency maneuver by Martin Frost (D–TX) then triggered a reconsideration of the amendment that defeated it on another voice vote. The subsequent roll call saw the Republicans unexpectedly abstaining for the most part, with several known enemies of the amendment voting for it. Four Democrats who had spoken in behalf of Synar-Obey from the floor were put in the embarrassing position of having to either vote against it or abstain in order to prevent it from becoming a "bill-killer." The amendment was defeated 126 to 122 with 156 members voting "present"; the Democratic bill then passed on a sharply partisan 255 to 155 vote. The Republican alternative—which would have cut maximum PAC contributions by 80 percent, required candidates to raise at least half of their money from constituents, and tilted the system in favor of party spending—had been rejected by a 241 to 169 margin earlier in the day.

When the Congress reconvened after its August and Labor Day recess, two events—the Persian Gulf crisis and the budget-deficit crisis—

consumed both houses. A House-Senate Conference Committee consisting of twelve senators and twenty-eight representatives—representing a wide variety of views beyond the elections commiteees—was appointed. A Republican effort in the House failed by a vote of 225 to 194 to instruct the conferees to accept several anti-PAC and antifranking provisions in the Senate bill. The large membership of the Conference Committee made any effort to get a quorum difficult, and, in fact, it never met.[68]

REASONS FOR THE FAILURE OF FEDERAL REFORM

In the spring of 1990, Representative Mike Synar was asked why Congress was having so much trouble reforming its system of campaign finance. "It's not that members can't be objective," the Oklahoman explained. "It's the fact we have 535 'experts' who think they know exactly the best thing to do to change the present system." With so little prospect for accord, why was the effort being made? Synar's reply was obvious: "It's clear that Americans have a high level of disgust for us."[69]

Campaign finance is a politician's issue; along with redistricting, it is the lifeblood of most members of Congress. Though concerned about increasing amounts of time spent raising funds, members have come to view election reform attempts as partisan maneuvers designed to exploit their party's strengths and their rivals' weaknesses. Those members with their ears to the ground, however, also have realized that the constant politician-bashing by the media on campaign fund-raising ethics has taken its toll. They felt compelled to stage at least a lively debate over the issue. Subsequently, each party made a dash for the popular high ground: Democrats by emphasizing the containment of campaign costs, Republicans by savaging PACs and nonparty soft money.

Though enough cooperation was established to enable each chamber to pass its own dissimilar, Democratic-oriented bill, the products of their labor were treated with a certain lack of seriousness. A telling example was provided by the normally compliant federal bureaucracy: After the passage of S 137 by the Senate, the Federal Election Commission refused a request from the Office of Management and Budget for an estimate of what the bill would cost. The likelihood of the measure ever becoming law was so remote that the FEC considered such an exercise to be a waste of time.[70]

The whole convoluted dance of political finance reform, which consumed so much attention on Capitol Hill from 1987 to 1990, might all be considered a waste of time were it not for the public relations value and political mileage that Congress was ultimately able to wring from the issue. For rather than make the public interest the guiding light behind the reform legislation—trading off partisan concerns about various particulars as the package was constructed—legislative strategists chose instead to immunize their proposals from adoption by potential allies across the aisle. Once safely insulated from any possibility of actually enacting a law, both Democratic and Republican parliamentary maneuvers stuffed bills with popular reform ideas, regardless of their legitimate merit or constitutional appropriateness.

The Democratic leadership in the House, firmly in control of the legislative process in that body, seems never to have seriously considered anything but a strongly partisan bill. The provisions to curb PACs in HR 5400 were plainly designed to leave the political operations of organized labor alone, a reflection of their overwhelming support for Democratic candidates. Corporate and trade committees split their money rather evenly, mainly because the Democrats control Congress; their basic inclination has historically been Republican. Consequently, the House action sought to retain their support.

The same partisan prejudices are evident in those provisions of HR 5400 directed at the party organizations. Constraints on the use of soft money by the parties would have been sharply tightened, and nonparty soft expenditures—chiefly practiced by labor unions—were untouched. The bill also proposed restricting nominees to accepting only $5,000 from all state party organizations combined, rather than $5,000 from each. It hardly seems coincidental to note that Republicans have a much stronger party infrastructure already in place for raising and distributing cash or that unions make substantial soft campaign expenditures, almost all in behalf of Democratic candidates.[71]

Chastened by their humbling experience with S 2 in the 100th Congress, the Senate Democratic leadership showed far more ambition for reaching a bipartisan accord in the deliberations of 1990. In the end, however, these limited accommodations succeeded only in securing senators a platform on the floor and roll call votes with which to exhibit a proreform stance to the voters.

It is remarkable how close accord appeared to be at various points in the spring and early summer of 1990. Where the spirit for enacting serious reform broke down is difficult to establish, but it seems that the July 4 congressional recess reoriented the thinking of many members. Two priorities quickly became paramount to lawmakers: Give all appearances of trying to clean up the system, but accomplish nothing that might threaten electoral security. Subsequently, the Democrats loaded their S 137 package with all manner of reforms that had been touted by the reformers' lobby (many of them ill-advisedly), convinced that the bill's severe spending limits would force President Bush to play the heavy and kill it. Eventually, concern bubbled over in the

Democratic caucuses of both houses that their professed wishes might somehow come true, and an embarrassed leadership was forced to add measures that were designed to protect incumbents even further.

The process gradually wore down the credibility of the legislation to the point where Senator Pat Moynihan was playing populist with it to the amusement of many. Along the way, provisions were tacked on without proper research on their feasibility or without regard to the constitutional issues they raised. One would have required the FEC to provide the treasury secretary with estimates on how much public funding each Senate candidate would be entitled to receive. But the report was to be due on January 1 of the election year, long before many such candidacies would even be declared; it would be impossible at that point to determine whether or not a campaign would even be eligible for public subsidies, much less be asesssed for the amount.[72]

The Democratic leadership in the Senate—Boren and Mitchell— were out of tune with the mainstream of Democratic senators but were able to forge a far-reaching bill nevertheless, particularly in its anti-PAC provisions.

The Senate bill was especially irresponsible with regard to First Amendment rights in its attempts to emasculate negative advertising and derail the independent expenditure protections extended by *Buckley* v. *Valeo*, both of which usually work to the net disadvantage of incumbents. Candidates would have been required to make a full-screen appearance on each of their television ads and declare, "I am a candidate for [name of office] and I approved the contents of this broadcast." If candidates had refused to abide by the "voluntary" spending limits, they would have been required to add that fact to their televised mea culpa as well. Independent expenditure campaigns would have been countered with public funds given to the opponent of the candidate they espoused, and their television advertising would have been saddled with the onerous burden of having a disclaimer fill a quarter of the screen throughout the commercial, then narrated at the conclusion—lest any voters be confused.[73]

Such provisions—which appeared to have been written with no responsible campaign experience or concern for constitutional law— belie contentions that S 137 was crafted in a serious effort to legislate reform. It is little wonder the FEC or, for that matter, the White House regarded the finished product as a political exercise.

Not that Republicans were blameless for the failure of reform: Throughout the long legislative process, they steadfastly made enhancing the influence of party apparatuses and diminishing the influence of labor unions the hallmark of their proposals and negotiating positions. As much as the Democrats, the Republicans sought to maximize their partisan advantages and minimize the resources of their adversaries, appealing to popular notions of reform whenever possible—even when such notions were plainly misconceived or impossible to attain. And the role of President Bush and the White House staff was prominent throughout but mainly because of a premature announcement in July that the president would veto any legislation containing public funding or spending limits.[74]

Another failure can be laid at the feet of the public interest lobby and editorial writers across the country who echoed the reformers and helped to misdirect the cause of campaign finance reform by fostering the perception that mixing private funds with the electoral process results in moral corruption. Their "all or nothing" stance, it can be argued, prevented any incremental improvements through the eleven years since the 1979 amendments, on grounds that minor change would ensure that public financing and spending limits would not be enacted.

The alternative view sees money in politics not as inherent evil but rather as a requirement if democracy is to function properly. If overly restricted, special interest and PAC money will find new channels to filter into the system one way or another; accordingly, the least offensive approach, both constitutionally and practically, is to permit it via PACs in ways that are open and disclosed. More money properly spent on campaigns equates to more voters informed of their choices in greater depth, more interest generated in political discourse, and more motivation aroused to travel to the polls and vote. If the money is raised in a widely dispersed fashion—modest donations from great numbers of people—political interest and involvement on a large scale is further enhanced, and the system becomes more of a reflection of the popular will—the function of democracy. For example, tax credits for political contributions can be structured to act as incentives to wider contributions, perhaps through benefits only to in-state contributors of limited amounts, as the Senate Campaign Finance Reform Panel suggested.

By insisting on the limitation of campaign spending, the reform coalition has provided cover for a Congress that is less than anxious to pursue reform. Democrats have been able to set proposed limits so low the Republicans could never accept them; Republicans have been able to cite the public financing required for compliance with limits and declare it another Democratic raid on the treasury. Each side has been able to point a finger of blame at the other and yet claim to be a reform advocate.

What the Congress has never seriously considered is a system of "floors without ceilings." Some supporters of public funding advocate public funding floors without spending limit ceilings. This concept is favored by many of the mature democracies in Western Europe; the idea is that partial public funding, or a floor, gives candidates (or in Western Europe, parties) at least minimal access to the electorate and provides alternative funds so that candidates (or parties) can reject undesirable private contributions. If this approach were accepted by the Congress, the absence of spending limits would avoid the constitutional issues raised in the *Buckley* case. Although this system appears to favor incumbents who have an advantage in raising funds, the floors actually assist challengers by providing them with money, thereby giving them some degree of access to the voting public.

Floors without ceilings were actually experienced in the presidential general elections of 1988, when public funds provided the floors but the ceilings or expenditure limits were not effective because of substantial soft money spending. It took from 1976 to 1988 for soft money to break out significantly, but the lesson is that as the system evolves, ceilings eventually collapse. Ensuring that all serious contenders have a reasonable minimum is more important than limiting how much candidates can spend. The bigger problem is how to provide money to candidates, not how to unduly restrict it. Some such formula would serve both parties well: Democrats would get public funding, and Republicans would not be burdened with expenditure limits.

A truly effective and well-directed public interest lobby would concentrate its efforts on legislation that would encourage a broader donor base (perhaps through tax credits for small contributions from constituents), maximize candidate competition, lower the cost of campaign communications, strengthen political parties, and broaden public disclosure of campaign activities. Its strategy would recognize partisan interests and balance them in winning concessions for the democratic process, exposing legislative theatrics and retreats from reform rather than excusing them.

For editorial writers to espouse "freedom of the press" while seeking to limit political spending—the voicing of political ideas—is ironic. Both electronic and print media would prefer to frame the campaigns to the electorate in their own words rather than allow candidates to speak for themselves, even if through the unpopular spot announcements that candidates find effective. But no one seems to point out that elections are improved by well-financed candidates able to wage competitive campaigns, not by stifling political dialogue.

Reform of federal campaign finance practices can and should be made to better promote the democratic process, but opportunities to do so are too frequently lost. Perhaps the public outcry against the current system has reached its crescendo. If the savings and loan affair cannot spur reform legislation, what can?

Despite these gloomy perceptions, the outlook for reform remains bright. There is a strong foundation left by the congressional efforts of 1987–1990. Both the Senate and House have now gone on record as favoring a number of policy changes that would be helpful: opening soft money to greater scrutiny, curbing the franking privilege (particularly in election years), and eliminating honoraria. A consensus appears to be present for requiring broadcast stations to cut political advertising costs. And House honoraria and the ability to convert campaign funds to personal use are due to pass from existence in 1991.

Momentum for a meaningful democratic reform of campaign financing has been generated and may be sustained by continuing investigations into the linkage between the savings and loan disaster and campaign contributions. Federal reform efforts will remain stymied, however, if toleration continues for the pursuit of partisan agendas at the expense of public interest.

NOTES

1. "458 Million Spent by 1988 Congressional Campaigns," Federal Election Commission, press release, February 24, 1989.

2. Hendrik Hertzberg, "Twelve Is Enough," *New Republic,* May 14, 1990, p. 22.

3. Janet Hook, "New Drive to Limit Tenure Revives an Old Proposal," *Congressional Quarterly,* vol. 48, no. 8, February 24, 1990, pp. 567–569.

4. "Dole's Presidential Hopes Provide Target for S 2 Supporters," *Campaign Practices Reports,* vol. 14, no. 13, June 29, 1987, p. 3.

5. "Filibuster Threat Hangs over Campaign Financing Debate," *Congressional Quarterly,* vol. 45, no. 23, June 6, 1987, p. 1187. Also Senator Mitch McConnell, "Don't Make Taxpayers Finance Campaigns," op-ed, *Washington Post National Weekly Edition,* July 20, 1987, p. 29.

6. "Fifth Vote Fails to Cut Off Election-Funds Filibuster," *Los Angeles Times,* June 19, 1987.

7. "Senate Stymied over Campaign Finance Bill," *Campaign Practices Reports,* vol. 14, no. 12, June 15, 1987, p. 2.

8. "Dole's Presidential Hopes," op. cit.

9. Richard L. Berke, "Money and Politics: What Mix?" *New York Times,* June 23, 1987.

10. Karen Tumulty, "Campaign Finance Bill Stalled in Senate," *Los Angeles Times,* September 16, 1987.

11. "Perfuming Money in the Senate," *New York Times,* editorial, June 9, 1987; and "The Tin Cup Club," *Washington Post,* editorial, July 6, 1987.

12. Berke, op. cit.

13. "S 2 Shelved," *PACs & Lobbies,* July 1, 1987, pp. 1, 7.

14. "Senate Seeks Compromise on Campaign Finance Bill," *Campaign Practices Reports,* vol. 15, no. 4, February 22, 1988, p. 2.

15. David S. Cloud, "Campaign-Finance Bill Snagged on Partisanship," *Congressional Quarterly,* vol. 46, no. 11, March 12, 1988, p. 2.

16. Janet Hook, "Packwood Arrested, Carried into Chamber," *Congressional Quarterly,* vol. 46, no. 9, February 27, 1988, p. 487.

17. David S. Cloud, "Senate Declines New Approach to Limiting Campaign Finances," *Congressional Quarterly,* vol. 46, no. 17, April 23, 1988, p. 1108.

18. "Senate to Vote on Constitutional Amendment Allowing Limits on Campaign Spending," *Campaign Practices Reports,* vol. 15, no. 7, April 4, 1988, pp. 1–3.

19. James J. Kilpatrick, "The 5 Senators and Charlie Keating," *Washington Post,* November 2, 1989.

20. "It's a Wonderful Life: S & L Investments on Capitol Hill," Common Cause study, Washington, D.C., June 1990.

21. Alan Secrest, "A Year of Living Dangerously," *Polling Report,* July 23, 1990, p. 8.

22. Hertzberg, op. cit.

23. Robin Toner, "House Edgy as Elections Loom and Voters Glower," *New York Times,* August 5, 1990.

24. Larry J. Sabato, *PAC Power: Inside the World of Political Action Committees* (New York: W. W. Norton & Co., 1985), p. 75.

25. "Campaign Reform," press release dated September 22, 1989, from the office of U.S. Representative Guy Vander Jagt (R–MI), cochair of the Bipartisan Task Force on Campaign Reform.

26. "Search for a Cure," *National Journal,* vol. 22, no. 24, June 16, 1990, p. 1484.

27. Peter Osterlund, "Panel Unveils Campaign Finance Plan," *Baltimore Sun,* March 8, 1990.

28. Campaign Finance Reform Panel, "Campaign Finance Reform: A Report to the Majority Leader and Minority Leader, United States Senate," March 6, 1990.

29. Kim Mattingly, " 'Flexible Spending Limits' Pique Interest of Leaders," *Roll Call,* March 8, 1990.

30. Helen Dewar, " 'Flexible' Campaign Spending Limits Suggested," *Washington Post,* March 8, 1990; David S. Broder, "Campaign Finance Reform: Keep It on Track," *Washington Post,* March 14, 1990; "Closing in on Campaign Reform," *Washington Post,* March 12, 1990; "The Senate's Honor," *New York Times,* May 13, 1990.

31. Richard E. Cohen, "Back Room Bargaining," *National Journal,* vol. 22, no. 11, March 17, 1990, pp. 672–673.

32. Chris Harvey, "GOP Hopes Bolstered on Campaign Reform," *Washington Times,* March 8, 1990.

33. Bill Whalen, "Spring Fever for Campaign Reform," *Insight,* April 2, 1990, p. 22.

34. Ibid.

35. Chris Harvey, "Democrats Embrace Flexible Spending Caps," *Washington Times,* April 23, 1990.

36. Helen Dewar, "Flexible Limits Offered as Campaign-Finance Compromise," *Washington Post*, March 8, 1990. Also, Harvey, "GOP Hopes Bolstered," op. cit.

37. "Time for Campaign Reform," *Washington Post*, editorial, May 29, 1990.

38. Commission for the Study of the American Electorate, "A Study of Campaign Expenses of Winning Challengers for Senate and House 1978–1988," released by the commission on May 17, 1990. Also, interview by Herbert Alexander with Curtis Gans, July 1990.

39. Chuck Alston, "The Maze of Spending Limits: An Election Field Guide," *Congressional Quarterly*, vol. 48, no. 21, May 26, 1990, p. 1621.

40. David Beiler, "DNC Plans Hit Summer Doldrums," *Campaigns & Elections*, vol. 11, no. 2, June/July 1990, pp. 9–10.

41. Federal Election Commission, *Federal Elections '86* (Washington, D.C.: Federal Election Commission, 1987), pp. 3–7.

42. Richard L. Berke, "Altered Campaign Bill Aids Senators," *New York Times*, May 11, 1990.

43. "Senate Debates Campaign Reform in Secret," *PACs & Lobbies*, June 6, 1990, pp. 1–2.

44. Chuck Alston, "Negotiators Tread Carefully to Find Common Ground," *Congressional Quarterly*, vol. 48, no. 21, May 26, 1990, p. 1627.

45. Richard L. Berke, "Senate Campaign Finance Talks Break Down," *New York Times*, June 17, 1990.

46. Alston, "The Maze of Spending Limits" op. cit., p. 1622.

47. Chuck Alston, "Campaign Finance: Rancorous Floor Action Looms in House as Well as Senate," *Congressional Quarterly*, vol. 48, no. 25, June 23, 1990, p. 1936.

48. Tom Kenworthy, "Campaign Finance Plan Drawing Fire in House," *Washington Post*, June 20, 1990.

49. "Is It Too Late for Congress to Act on Campaign Reform?" *PACs & Lobbies*, July 4, 1990, p. 2.

50. Alston, "Campaign Finance," op. cit.

51. Secrest, op. cit., p. 1.

52. Tom Kenworthy, "Democrats Rip Common Cause," *Washington Post*, July 13, 1990.

53. Ibid.

54. Steven A. Holmes, "Weaker Limit on PACs Is Proposed," *New York Times*, July 31, 1990.

55. Robert P. Hey, "Congress to Consider Campaign Reforms," *Christian Science Monitor*, June 5, 1990.

56. Holmes, op. cit.

57. Helen Dewar, "Senate Democrats Accept Republican Proposal to Outlaw PACs," *Washington Post*, July 28, 1990. Also, Chuck Alston, "Showdown on Spending Limits Moves to White House," *Congressional Quarterly*, vol. 48, no. 31, August 4, 1990, p. 2481.

58. Alston, "Showdown on Spending Limits," op. cit.

59. Matt Yancey, "Reform Bipartisanship Disappears, Republicans Complain," Associated Press wire, August 1, 1990.

60. Chuck Alston, "Campaign Finance Measures," *Congressional Quarterly,* vol. 48, no. 32, August 11, 1990, p. 2618.

61. Martin Tolchin, "U.S. May Prohibit Foreign-tied PACs," *New York Times,* July 4, 1990; also see Roger Wolk and David C. Huckabee, "PACs Sponsored by Corporations Partly or Wholly Owned by Foreign Investors," CRS Report 89–618 GOV, Congressional Research Service, Washington, D.C., November 14, 1989.

62. Alston, "Showdown on Spending Limits," op. cit., p. 2479.

63. Richard L. Berke, "Senate Votes to Curb Donations from Outside Groups," *New York Times,* August 2, 1990.

64. Richard L. Berke, "Campaign Surgery," *New York Times,* August 5, 1990.

65. Tom Kenworthy, "House Passes Campaign Finance Reform Package," *Washington Post,* August 4, 1990.

66. Kim Mattingly, "House Disposes of Campaign Reform Bill," *Roll Call,* August 6, 1990.

67. Tom Kenworthy, "Campaign Bill Causes Revolt by Democrats," *Washington Post,* August 2, 1990.

68. "House-Senate Conferees: All Dressed Up but Nowhere to Go," *PACs & Lobbies,* October 3, 1990, p. 5.

69. Dan Fesperman, "While Congressmen Spit Fire, Re-election War Chests Fill Up," *Baltimore Sun,* April 25, 1990. Also, "Running for Cover," *Newsweek,* August 13, 1990, p. 32.

70. Walter Pincus, "Flaws Cited in the Senate's Campaign Finance Bill," *Washington Post,* August 19, 1990.

71. Peter Osterlund, "Partisan Politics Stymies Election Financing Reform," *Baltimore Sun,* August 25, 1990.

72. Pincus, "Flaws Cited," op. cit.

73. Ibid.

74. Executive Office of the President, "Statement of Administration Policy," July 31, 1990.

APPENDIX
AMENDING THE FEDERAL ELECTION CAMPAIGN ACT: A STATEMENT OF RECOMMENDATIONS BY FORMER PRESIDENTIAL CAMPAIGN FINANCE OFFICERS

I. THE BACKGROUND

On December 9, 1988, some 17 persons who served as finance chairmen, directors or treasurers of the major presidential campaigns in 1988 or who took part in fund raising on behalf of the campaigns or the political parties met in Washington, D.C., under the auspices of the Citizens' Research Foundation. These experts and additional selected observers analyzed the impact of the Federal Election Campaign Act and its amendments on the conduct of the 1988 presidential prenomination and general election campaigns. Their goal was to arrive at a consensus regarding any changes they deemed necessary in the laws that regulate presidential campaign financing.

Prior to the conference, each participant received a copy of a background paper authored by conference chairman Herbert E. Alexander. The paper summarized presidential campaign finance law and posed a series of questions for consideration by the participants.

At the conference itself, participants were divided into four task forces, each concentrating its attention on one of four areas of presidential campaign finance regulation: contribution limits, expenditure limits, public funding and public disclosure, including compliance with and enforcement of the law. Each task force developed a series of proposals in its area of examination. All conference participants had an opportunity to discuss, amend and vote on all the proposals in a plenary session that concluded the conference.

Following the conference, the amended proposals were mailed to all conference participants for their response. In order to involve as many interested presidential campaign finance officers as possible, the proposals also were mailed to persons who had been invited to participate in the conference but were unable to do so. Recipients were asked to indicate their support for or opposition to each proposal and to comment on the proposals if they felt it useful. The results of this process are incorporated in the Statement of Recommendations.

The Citizens' Research Foundation is a non-profit, non-partisan organization devoted exclusively to studying political finance and disseminating information about this important subject to the public. The Foundation gratefully acknowledges the support it received to convene the 1988 Presidential Finance Officers Conference from the following sponsors: Arie and Ida Crown Memorial, W. Averell and Pamela C. Harriman Foundation, Ethel and Philip Klutznick Charitable Trusts, The Norman Lear Foundation, and Manning J. Post.

The proposals made in the Statement of Recommendations represent the views of the conference participants who endorsed the statement and not necessarily the positions of the Citizens' Research Foundation trustees or members of its council of advisors or of the sponsors that provided support for the conference.

II. A STATEMENT OF RECOMMENDATIONS

The following proposals received support of 75 percent or more of those who participated in the conference evaluating laws that regulate presidential campaign financing. The undersigned believe that the following proposals merit prompt action.

1. While there was considerable sentiment to repeal contribution limits entirely, it was recognized that what may be politically feasible would be to raise the individual limit to $5,000 and adjust annually for inflation, rounding out to the nearest $100 increment. This change would take into account the effect of inflation since 1974 on the current $1,000 limit, requiring in 1988 some $2,246.18 to purchase what $1,000 bought in 1975 when the limit went into effect. This recommendation recognizes the excessive time candidates need to devote to fund raising, and candidates' need for seed money to mount competitive campaigns. A $5,000 contribution, or even an unlimited contribution, to a presidential prenomination campaign is unlikely to give the contributor undue influence in the nomination process, particularly since public disclosure assures that voters will know the sources of all large contributors.

2. Raise the aggregate $25,000 limit per calendar year on contributions by an individual to federal election campaigns, to at least $50,000 or more to match proportionally the contribution limit increase. Raising the limit would make more money available to candidates, and it might reduce the felt need for expenditures of "soft money." The amounts should be indexed for inflation and rounded to the nearest $100.

3. Permit a donor to contribute during the post-election period only, for compliance purposes only, up to an additional $5,000, above and beyond the limits imposed during the campaign period or the calendar year.

4. Raise the amount of the presidential pre-nomination campaign spending limit by $10 million based on 1988 levels ($23.1 million) and continue to adjust the expenditure limit according to changes in the Consumer Price Index. However, the current 20 percent overage for fund-raising costs would be retained and calculated from the new base, $33.1 million, and adjusted according to changes in the CPI. In the absence of a more acceptable alternative, an overall spending limit serves the need of preventing inordinate spending.

5. Continue to provide public matching funds to eligible candidates for presidential nomination. Continue to require candidates for presidential nomination to qualify for public matching funds by raising a minimum of $5,000 in each of 20 states through contributions from individuals of $250 or less. This procedure helps assure that only politically viable candidates receive public funds. In order to ease the fund-raising burden on candidates and to cope with frontloading and primary and caucus concentrations on a given date, raise the maximum matchable amount for an individual contribution to a candidate for presidential nomination from $250 to $500 but continue to limit the aggregate amount of matching funds a candidate may receive to 50 percent of the national spending limit. Maintain the current 1-to-1 ratio of matching funds to individual contributions.

6. Retain the personal and family expenditure limit at the $50,000 amount as at present. This limit applies to combined expenditures during the prenomination and general election campaigns.

7. Eliminate individual state spending limits in presidential prenomination contests. These limits have proven to be unrealistic and unenforceable.

8. Change the starting date for receiving matching funds from January 1 of the election year to July 1 of the year preceding the election, and change eligibility to count contributions for matching funds to 18 months prior to the election year. These changes are designed to enable candidates to receive public funding during part of the year preceding the election because the start-up costs of a presidential campaign are enormous.

9. Eligibility to receive matching funds should survive the death or withdrawal of the candidate, in order to enable staff to work to pay off any debts.

10. Retain the federal income tax checkoff to provide public funds for presidential campaigns. In order to ensure adequate public funding under recommendation Numbers 4, 5, and 8, raise the amount that taxpayers may earmark for the Presidential Election Campaign Fund from $1 to $3 on individual returns and from $2 to $6 on joint returns.

11. Restructure Federal Election Commission audit procedures to reflect fewer expected challenges once state-by-state expenditure limits are repealed. This will permit more FEC focus on receipts during the audit process, and may conclude the audit process sooner.

12. Maintain at the current level the existing system of funding presidential general election campaigns: 100 percent public funding for major-party nominees at the level established by the 1974 FECA Amendments; partial public funding for eligible independent, new party and minor-party presidential campaigns and providing public funds only to those independent, minor-party and new-party candidates who have demonstrated significant support. Moreover, this system fosters party building by encouraging individuals who want to participate financially in the major-party presidential campaigns to contribute to national party committees which may use a specified amount of the funds received to pay for permissible coordinated party expenditures on behalf of their presidential tickets.

13. Eliminate restrictions on the political parties' use of their presidential nominees' names in connection with all fund-raising and party-building activities.

14. As evidenced by the public funding, the coordinated spending by the national parties, and the uses of soft money, presidential general election campaigns are very expensive. A strong consensus favors encouraging broadcasters to provide presidential candidates in both the pre- and post-nomination phases of the presidential selection process more free time and more certain access to free and bought time. Improvements in the system of lowest unit rate are necessary in order to reduce candidate campaign costs.

15. The raising of soft money should be encouraged but in the name of political party committees, not the fund-raising apparatuses of the nominated candidates. A system of disclosure of soft money should be developed to include reporting of all national party non-federal accounts, the mandating of federal disclosure requirements if state laws remain inadequate, and mandating disclosure by state and local party committees of all out-of-state receipts. The need is for disclosure of all major soft money gifts at least one month prior to the election. The undersigned renew the recommendations made four years ago by a similar group:

> Develop a centralized procedure at the national level to collect and make available information regarding contributions and expenditures of "soft money" by analyzing the conduits through which such money is channeled to state and local levels to pay for activities to benefit presidential campaigns. Define clearly the types of contributions and expenditures to be analyzed. Coordinate procedures for gathering and disseminating information with state and local campaign reporting offices.

16. Reporting and disclosure should be geared to a level which provides maximum public information about the financing of political campaigns but does not inhibit broad-based participation in the process by political parties, candidates and individuals. Where disclosure is unduly com-

plicated it should be narrowed and simplified to encourage participation and reduce costs to campaigns. There are a variety of accounting systems in use, some of which are cumbersome. Accordingly, the FEC should be required to recommend use of a standard software program to be used by political committees. In the absence of a commercially developed program available at inexpensive rates, the FEC should develop one for widespread use. Any other programs should be able to be converted to the standard one adopted. Subject the campaign law's reporting requirements to a continuing cost-benefit analysis to determine whether the reporting burdens of candidates and political committees result in commensurate public benefit.

17. Require the FEC to develop and make available facilities permitting electronic transmission of financial reports to the FEC. Some envisage a future in which all reporting is transmitted electronically on a daily basis using identical programming.

18. Require a better definition of collateralization for candidate and committee loans to ensure that indebtedness not be used as a means to avoid expenditure limits.

19. The undersigned urge an increase in efforts to achieve greater electoral participation in terms of registration, voting, volunteer service to parties and candidates, and contributing money. A public education campaign should be designed and implemented. If costs are significant, an increase in the tax checkoff amount earmarked for these purposes is recommended.

Endorsers of Presidential Finance Officers' Statement

Charles Black (Kemp)
E. Mark Braden (Former Chief Counsel, Republican National Committee)
William E. Brock (Republican National Committee)
Kristin Demong (Dukakis)*
Duane B. Garrett (Babbitt)
Jules Glazer (Jackson)
Kenneth A. Gross (several campaigns)
Nancy Jacobson (Gore)
Fred Karger (Committee for the Presidency)
M. Larry Lawrence (Democratic National Committee)
Boyd B. Lewis (Gephardt)
Terence R. McAuliffe (Gephardt)
Michael P. Novelli (Hart)
Robert P. Odell (Bush)
Douglas A. Rediker (Dukakis)
Timothy L. Roper (Bush)
Philip S. Smith (Republican National Finance Committee)
Rodney A. Smith (Kemp)
Allan R. Sutherlin (Robertson)
William R. Sweeney, Jr. (Gore)

*With reservations

About the Book and Authors

What cost more than $2.7 billion and increased 50 percent over levels just four years earlier? Campaign-related spending during the 1987–1988 U.S. election cycle topped all previous records, not only in amount but also in ingenuity. The 1988 election saw the advent of a wide variety of political funding vehicles, some of which demonstrate the inventiveness of political actors in circumventing the laws of campaign finance and continue to provoke controversy and demands for further regulation. *Financing the 1988 Election* goes beyond totaling campaign expenditures to carefully document the sources of the money spent.

Alexander and Bauer treat campaign money as a tracer element that, when carefully tracked, reveals valuable information about people and patterns of political power. They describe in detail the role that money played in the campaigns of each of the major contenders for the 1988 presidential nomination and election and in congressional campaigns as well. Funding innovations and outlays—including the uses of soft money, independent expenditures, communication costs, and political broadcasting—are highlighted along the way.

By following the "money path," Alexander and Bauer shed light on often obscure aspects of the political process and contribute to our understanding of political influence and power in the United States. In an epilogue, Alexander offers a valuable update on congressional efforts to develop appropriate campaign finance reform legislation.

Financing the 1988 Election deserves a space on scholars' and students' shelves alike for its authoritative compilation of essential and telling data. It is applicable to a wide variety of American government courses, including campaigns and elections, parties, and public opinion.

Herbert E. Alexander is professor of political science at the University of Southern California and since 1958 has been the director of the Citizens'

Research Foundation. In 1990, he was a member of the Senate Campaign Finance Reform Panel. He has written numerous books on campaign finance including seven in this series on the financing of presidential election campaigns. **Monica Bauer** is assistant professor of government at Western New England College. Her work has appeared in the *American Journal of Political Science*.

INDEX